The Interpreters Training Manual for Museums

Mary Kay Cunningham

AMERICAN ASSOCIATION OF MUSEUMS

The Interpreters Training Manual for Museums

On the cover: Young girl and *The Dancers* by George Segal. National Gallery of Art, Gallery Archives. © Dennis Brack/Black Star.

Design: LevineRiederer Design

Library of Congress Cataloging-in-Publication Data
Cunningham, Mary Kay.
  The interpreter's training manual for museums / Mary Kay Cunningham.
    p. cm.
  Includes bibliographical references and index.
  ISBN 0-931201-90-X
  1. Museums—Educational aspects—Handbooks, manuals, etc. 2. Museums—Educational aspects—United States—Handbooks, manuals, etc. 3. Museums—Employees—Training of—United States—Handbooks, manuals, etc. 4. Museum curators—Training of—United States—Handbooks, manuals, etc. 5. Museum visitors—Educational aspects—United States—Handbooks, manuals, etc. 6. Tour guides (Persons)—Training of—United States—Handbooks, manuals, etc. 7. Volunteer workers in museums—Training of—United States—Handbooks, manuals, etc. 8. Educators—United States—Handbooks, manuals, etc. I. Title.
  AM7.C86 2004
  069'.15—dc22
                                            2004014829

The Interpreters Training Manual for Museums

Table of Contents

MODULE 2: APPLYING INTERACTIVE TECHNIQUES TO INTERACTIVE OPPORTUNITIES

MODULE 3: DEVELOPING NEW INTERPRETIVE PROGRAMS

THE TOOLS OF INTERPRETATION

If education is about the negotiation of meaning and museums are a forum for that, then our definitions of the institution must begin to allow, first, for variation in meaning and, second, for interaction between presenters and participants.

Lisa Roberts • From Knowledge to Narrative: Education and the Changing Museum (1997)

Acknowledgements

I had no idea what I was getting myself into when I accepted a position with Lisa Roberts in the public programs department of the Chicago Botanic Garden in 1994. From day one, I was encouraged to think about "what makes a meaningful visitor experience" and "how to maximize the learning narrative between interpreters and visitors." Ten years later it isn't hard to see how I became inspired to pursue strategies for training interpreters to facilitate these meaningful experiences. I would like to thank Lisa and others who have served as professional mentors, collaborators, reviewers, and friends as I have pursued this work, including Stephanie Weaver, Tracy McClendon, Cheryl Main, Tina Nolan, Doug Widener, Melanie Napoleon, Nicole Royal, Erik Holland, Dave Bucy, Zina Castanuela, Barbara Butler, Stephen Bell, John Buranosky, Lisa Abia-Smith, Wendy Abelmann, and Tania Hyatt-Evenson.

I also want to express my gratitude to the countless volunteers, education staff, and administrators at the Peggy Notebaert Nature Museum, Chicago Botanic Garden, Children's Museum of Indianapolis, Fairchild Tropical Garden, Oregon Historical Society, Santa Cruz Museum of Art and History, Arizona Sonora Desert Museum, and Desert Botanical Garden for inspiring and supporting the research for this book over the past 10 years.

Many professional organizations and individuals provided valuable information and experiences during my research, including the American Association of Botanic Gardens and Arboreta; the fabulous staff at the National Association for Interpretation; David Larsen, Dave Dahlen, Sandy Webber, and Robert Fudge of the National Park Service; university professors Sam Ham, Ron Zimmerman, Michael Gross, Tom Mullins, Marjorie Schwarzer, and Kris Morrissey; visitor studies specialists Deborah Perry and Marcella Wells; my graduate thesis committee at Northeastern Illinois University, including Tom Simpson, Robert Easton, and Mary Rice; the American Association of Museums, and my editor, Jane Lusaka, for the good humor and persistent questioning that helped to clarify my thoughts and navigate the publishing experience.

Most important, I want to acknowledge those closest to me for giving me the strength and encouragement to pursue my passion. In many ways, this book would not have been possible without my amazing family: my parents, siblings, and their significant others all have reminded me that persistence, patience, love, and laughter go a long way towards accomplishing a goal. I am also grateful to the members of the "greatest generation," Grandma Cunningham and Frank and June Sackton, who recognized my potential long before I did. Each member of my extended family—the Moeller family, Greta, Nancy and Steve, and many invaluable friends, especially Sara and Bill Race, Lara and Kevin Blackwell, and Kelly Shelton—has made personal contributions that cannot be adequately recognized in words. Thanks for keeping me positive and determined to share this information with others.

Above all, I am indebted to my partner, Dan Moeller, who has unconditionally supported my efforts. It's a gift to have someone who challenges me to do things that matter, to take time for myself, and who reliably appears with champagne to inspire me whenever I want to give up. Thanks for believing in me.

Mary Kay Cunningham
April 2004

Truth is not in the conclusions so much as in the process of conversation itself.

Parker Palmer • "Good Teaching: A Matter of Living the Mystery"
(1990)

Introduction

More than 12,000 parks, museums, camps, zoos, gardens, and other educational sites in the United States have interpreters (Knudson, Cable, and Beck, 1995)—i.e., individuals who serve in a front-line role and facilitate positive and educational visitor experiences. In fact, estimates provided by the American Association for Museum Volunteers and the Association for Volunteer Administration indicate that almost 500,000 volunteers and docents serve in such a capacity at museums and similar sites.

However, despite the growing number of professional interpreters, as well as research that suggests that more than 90 percent of museums are offering docent training (Sachatello-Sawyer, et al., 2002), the literature dedicated to *helping* museums develop interpreter training is limited. Published works that elaborate on the virtues of interpretation's philosophy and methodology often lack the concise and practical learning tools sought by novice trainers and interpreters. Furthermore, my personal observations and research tell me that museum training programs tend to teach facts about sites or collections rather than explore the interpretive techniques that encourage visitors to actively engage in learning.

Over the years, I have talked with museum colleagues who have lamented the lack of support materials for training interpreters. How do we train our interpreters, they've asked, to facilitate personalized interactions that enhance the visitor experience? *The Interpreters Training Manual for Museums* is both a response to and product of those conversations. It is a comprehensive resource that shows both staff and volunteer interpreters how to engage visitors in a meaningful, message-based dialogue. Suitable for all types of museums—including botanical gardens, zoos, parks, and living history sites—this book establishes a practical and easy-to-follow framework for interpreter training through the use of group exercises, written and oral activities, interactive lectures, presentation tools, and opportunities to practice learned skills. Its goal is to help museum staff develop a progressive training program that references current educational learning theory and museum studies while modeling conversational interactions between museum visitor and interpreter. By enhancing and personalizing the experience for visitors, museums are more likely to maintain the ongoing public support they need to survive.

AN EVOLVING DEFINITION

In some circles, interpretation is considered a relatively new profession. Over time, it has moved from lecture-based *presentation* toward an interactive *exchange* of ideas between visitors and interpreters. Two publications, *Adventures of a Nature Guide and Essays in Interpretation* by Enos Mills (1920) and *Interpreting Our Heritage* by Freeman Tilden (1957) generally are recognized as the foundation of the field. Inspired by a close relationship with naturalist John Muir and a strong connection to the natural world, Mills saw the interpreter as someone "who can guide others to the secrets of nature." He wrote: "It is not necessary for a guide to be a walking encyclopedia. He arouses interest by dealing in big principles—not with detached and colorless information." Tilden built on this idea, defining interpretation as "an educational activity, which aims to reveal meanings and relationships through the use of original objects, by firsthand experience, and by illustrative media rather than simply to communicate factual information."

Today, however, uncertainty still surrounds the definition and application of interpretation at many institutions. Although relevant to all museums, Tilden's work is regularly referenced in environmental interpretation settings (e.g., parks, nature centers, natural areas), while more traditional museum settings (art and history institutions) are less likely to apply these time-tested lessons. As the needs of visitors and all museums (those with living collections and those without) evolve and expand, so, too, will the definition of interpretation. At a minimum, visitor studies suggest that interpretation should promote social interaction in an effort to personalize and enhance the museum visitor's learning experience. Engaging visitors in a meaningful dialogue encourages them to participate in their own learning and to develop deeper connections to the institution.

CONVERSATION AS INTERPRETATION

The idea of incorporating dialogue into educational practice is not new. Inquiry-based learning and the educational theories of constructivism, cooperative learning, and experience-based learning all advocate using dialogue in education. Constructivism serves as a foundation for message-based conversations because it emphasizes tapping the learner's previous knowledge to increase the effectiveness of the lesson. As suggested by the very word "constructivism," conversational interpreters are trained to help visitors rediscover what they already know about a subject and then *build* upon that foundation with new knowledge and experiences. "For museums," George Hein noted in his 1995 article, "The Constructivist Museum," "this translates into the dictum that we need to focus on the visitor, not the content of the museum."

In an essay titled "Elegant Programs and Conversations" in *Presence of Mind: Museums and the Spirit of Learning* (1999), Michael Spock cites several qualities that make personal interactions in museums meaningful:

They are mediated by people—live people. In contrast to the impersonal, fixed exhibit medium, programs and conversations derive their strength, flexibility, and connectedness from being human exercises. . . . Rather than being passive receptacles, the visitor contributes to, constructs, and helps create the visitor experience. . . . There is the assumption that the visitor or companion is not some poor soul in need of enlightenment, but a smart and capable collaborator. So it isn't that visitors are expected to work for their insights, but that they might actually have something to contribute to the exchange.

Building on these and other ideas, this manual focuses on showing interpreters how to improve and personalize the experience for their audiences and more effectively connect visitors to the museum's messages. The interpreters, collections, and messages may vary from site to site, but the elements and techniques of effective interpretation are universal.

Several objectives guided the development of this training manual. To be complete, *The Interpreters Training Manual for Museums* would need to:

1. offer a substantial and practical collection of resources and ideas for training interpreters

2. provide user-friendly tools and methods to help staff prepare and deliver interpretive training

3. offer information that appeals and applies to a variety of museums—those with living collections (e.g., botanic gardens, parks, zoos, aquariums) and those with non-living collections (e.g., art, history, natural history, science and technology)

4. reinforce the value of conversation and engaging visitors in a dialogue by providing sufficient background information on interpretation and related learning theory

5. offer the option of further investigation through additional resources (listed at the end of the book)

To that end, *The Interpreters Training Manual for Museums* adapts training materials from a variety of sources and disciplines, including communications and visitor studies, to show all professional staff, regardless of their interpretive expertise, how to offer a convenient, site-specific, and cost-effective training for interpreters. The book creates goals and expectations for the staff who will train full-time and volunteer interpreters; provides teaching outlines and exercises for implementing the training and evaluating trainees; and lists resources for enhancing and customizing interpretive training.

According to Ron Zimmerman, a professor at University of Wisconsin at Stevens Point— one of the few large U.S. universities with courses targeted at training interpreters—most interpreters working today don't have the benefit of formal training and rely on self-education and self-training (Zimmerman, 1999). Such a lack of formal training not only jeopardizes the credibility of the profession, but also prevents visitors from fully connecting with cultural, scientific, and natural sites (Veverka, 1998). As Senegalese naturalist Baba Dioum once said, "In the end, we protect only what we love, we love only what we understand, we understand only what we are taught." If we do not adequately train our interpreters to be effective educators, how can we expect them to teach visitors to love and respect our collections?

REFERENCES

Hein, George. 1995. "The Constructivist Museum." *Journal of Education in Museums*. 16: 21-23.

Mills, Enos. 1920. *Adventures of a Nature Guide and Essays on Interpretation*. Friendship, Wis.: New Past Press.

Knudson, D., Cable T. and L. Beck. 1995. *Interpretation of Cultural and Natural Resources*. State College, Pa.: Venture Publishing, Inc.

Palmer, Parker. 1990. "Good Teaching: A Matter of Living the Mystery." *Change* 22: 11-16.

Pitman, Bonnie, ed. 1999. *Presence of Mind: Museums and the Spirit of Learning*. Washington, D.C.: American Association of Museums.

Sachatello-Sawyer, Bonnie, et al. 2002. *Adult Museums Programs; Designing Meaningful Experiences*. Walnut Creek, Calif.: AltaMira Press.

Tilden, Freeman. 1957. *Interpreting Our Heritage*. Chapel Hill: University of North Carolina Press.

Veverka, John A. 1998. President of Veverka and Associates and author of *Interpretive Master Planning*. Phone interview, June 19, Evanston, Ill.

Zimmerman, Ron. 1999. Professor of interpretation, University of Wisconsin, Stevens Point; co-author of *The Interpreter's Guidebook*. Phone interview, March 20, Evanston, Ill.

How to Use This Manual

The Interpreters Training Manual for Museums is the result of comprehensive research and many years of experience in creating interpreter-training programs. A new approach to training interpreters, the book incorporates current learning theory and visitor studies that suggest that interaction and conversation are ideal ways to engage museum visitors in learning. The training materials were designed to adapt to the site-specific needs of all types of museums and make the task of training interpreters easier and more effective.

PREPARING FOR THE TRAINING

The first part of the manual creates goals and expectations for the training; serves as a checklist for the staff who will train full-time and volunteer interpreters; and enables those trainers to customize materials to meet the specific needs of their museums. Chapters 1 through 4 identify a series of tasks that must be completed by the trainer for the manual's goals to be met.

This section also addresses the preliminary phases of planning that can help an institution understand its mission, determine how it wants to define interpretation, and clarify the role of the interpreter in accomplishing its goals. Interpreter training cannot succeed unless the institution understands its current and target audience, which programs are effective, and the kinds of resources that will enhance the training. As with all good planning, if these early considerations are not addressed, subsequent pieces of the training will not be effective. Logistics also play a key role in creating a successful training program, and each chapter concludes with a set of forms—worksheets, sample documents, and other resources to help with this and all planning tasks. Some of these forms can be used as handouts for trainees (see chapter 20). Each form is labeled with a number, which references the chapter, and a *letter;* which indicates the form's placement at the end of the chapter. For example, worksheet 1A is the first form in chapter 1.

- **Worksheets** help the staff person (the trainer) and the interpreters (the trainees) consider and record useful information. They also serve as writing exercises that can help trainees process or apply various concepts.
- **Sample Documents** offer examples of recommended tools, such as job descriptions, evaluations, themes, and messages, and show how a concept or technique should be applied. Each trainer should adapt the content to best fit her institution.

THE TRAINING MODULES

The book includes three modules for interpretive training. Module 1 (chapters 5 to 10) provides trainees with an overview of interpretation and the factors that influence its effectiveness. Module 2 (chapters 11 to 14) clarifies how to engage visitors in site-specific interpretive conversations and structured programs. Module 3 (chapters 15 to 17) helps trainees create their own interpretive programs, integrating the lessons learned in the first two modules.

Dividing the training into three progressive modules allows organizations to adapt to the skill level and previous experiences of the interpreter trainees. This chart offers suggestions for how modules might be used with various groups of trainees.

Audience for Training	Module 1	Module 2	Module 3
Professional Interpreters	Highly relevant	Highly relevant	Relevant
Volunteer Interpreters	Highly relevant	Relevant	Moderately relevant
General Site Staff/Volunteers	Relevant	Moderately relevant	Not relevant

For instance, a full-time paid interpreter responsible for creating new programs should participate in Modules 1 through 3. But the first two modules would provide sufficient training for volunteer interpreters, who may not be in a position to create programs. Finally, staff and volunteers who interact with the public, such as those working in guest services, concessions, or security, will benefit from Module 1. This three-module structure helps staff members interact with the visitor in their specific roles and has been tested to ensure the greatest degree of effectiveness with each level of interpreter. Each trainer is encouraged to adapt and/or selectively use the book's materials to meet the specific needs of her institution.

TRAINING MANUAL FORMAT

In addition to training resources such as worksheets and sample documents, the training modules also provide overheads, exercises, and teaching outlines.

- **Overheads** provide a focal point and help the trainer supplement verbal instruction and dialogue. (The forms in this book can be photocopied onto overhead transparencies.)

- **Exercises** give trainees an opportunity to practice their skills among peers and encourage an open forum with an emphasis on dialogue. A list of required materials, props, or volunteer assistance precedes each exercise.

- **Training outlines** guide the trainer, step-by-step, through the training process, and tell the trainer when to use questions to facilitate discussion or the overheads, exercises, and worksheets to reinforce a concept.

Each module begins with a training outline, which includes a system of symbols to guide the trainer. For example, the symbol **()** indicates when a training exercise should occur. An 👁 indicates that there is an overhead that reinforces the lesson concept. A ✎ references a worksheet that can help trainees process ideas or techniques. In addition, questions that the trainer should ask the group are written in *italicized* text to emphasize the importance of group interaction.

Each module also includes a series of short, accessible chapters, which have been designed to provide enough background information to adequately inform trainers without overwhelming them.

THE TOOLS OF INTERPRETATION

The final section of the manual lists resources—publications, organizations, Web sites, and professional networks—with information on support for training programs and interpretive efforts in general. These materials may provide valuable new perspectives and ideas for interpretation. This section also includes a glossary, a list of sample handouts that trainers can photocopy for trainees, and an index of all the training tools for quick reference.

CHAPTER 1 • # Lay the Foundation: Establishing Your Interpretive Framework

Understanding the museum's mission and the role of interpretation in fulfilling that mission is the foundation of successful interpretive training. With that goal in mind, each trainer should complete these four tasks before the training begins:

1) REINFORCE OR DEFINE THE MUSEUM'S MISSION

A strong mission statement is a central part of a successful interpretive program. If a mission does not exist or needs to be redefined, the institution's leadership—in collaboration with staff and community members—must work to resolve the issue. Redefining or creating a mission statement involves two lines of questioning:

1. Who/what do we *think* we are? Who/what are we *in fact*? Who/what do we *want* to be?

2. Where do we *think* we are going? Where are we going in *fact*? Where do we *want* to go?

Answering these questions will help determine the institution's identity and direction—two vital components of a mission statement. It is important to define clearly the mission so that it can inform the interpretation process. Ideally, the mission will highlight the value of providing an engaging or interactive learning environment for visitors when it addresses what the museum does, as well as why and how it does it. Similarly, interpretation should reinforce the mission statement through interpretive planning and training programs. The mission creates expectations for both its staff and visitors. Given that most museums exist to serve their visitors in some capacity, the mission should outline the tone of the desired experience. Worksheet 1A contains an example and ideas for writing or refining a mission statement.

For guidance on creating or revising a mission statement, see *Museum Mission Statements: Building a Distinct Identity* (AAM, 2000) and the AAM Accreditation Commission's

Expectations Regarding Institutional Mission Statements, available at www.aam-us.org/programs/accreditation/mission.cfm.

2) DEFINE INTERPRETATION FOR YOUR SITE

A museum's definition of interpretation should reflect its unique character and institutional objectives (as stated in the mission). This definition will determine the tone and focus of all interpretive training and programs. While interpretation has its roots in the natural world, it can be applied to any setting. The following are some commonly referenced definitions of interpretation.

> A nature guide (interpreter) is a naturalist who can guide others to the secrets of nature. It is not necessary for them to be a walking encyclopedia. They arouse interest by dealing in big principles, not with detached and colorless information.
> Enos Mills, *Adventures of a Nature Guide*, 1920

> [Interpretation is an] educational activity which aims to reveal meanings and relationships through the use of original objects by first hand experience and illustrated media rather than simply to communicate factual information.
> Freeman Tilden, *Interpreting Our Heritage*, 1957

> Environmental Interpretation involves translating the technical language of a natural science or related field into terms and ideas that people who aren't scientists can understand.
> Sam Ham, *Environmental Interpretation*, 1992

> Interpretation is the process of making something understandable or of giving something a special meaning.
> Gary Edson and David Dean, *Handbook for Museums*, 1994

> Interpretation facilitates a connection between the interests of the visitor and the meanings of the resource.
> National Park Service, 1996

> Interpretation is the activities through which a museum carries out its mission and educational role; it is a dynamic communication between the museum and the audience; it is the means by which the museum delivers its content. Interpretive media/activities include, but are not limited to, exhibits, tours, Web sites, classes, school programs, publications, outreach.
> AAM's National Interpretation Project, 1999

> Interpretation is a communication process that forges emotional and intellectual connections between the interests of an audience and the inherent meanings in the resource.
> National Association for Interpretation, 2000

The definitions created by the National Park Service and the National Association of Interpretation (NAI) have been embraced by many interpretive professionals because they place great emphasis on making connections with visitors. In fact NAI's definition goes one step further by emphasizing the importance of both intellectual and emotional connections. If your organization is committed to the idea of conversation and dialogue with visitors, then incorporate that into your definition of interpretation. Then staff and volunteers will know that learning conversations are an institutional expectation. For example:

> Interpretation is conversation, guided interaction, or any communication that enriches the visitor experience by making meaningful connections between the messages and collections of our institution and the intellectual and emotional world of the visitor.

3) DETERMINE OR CLARIFY THE INTERPRETER'S ROLE IN THE INSTITUTION

It is important that trainers articulate the role that interpreters play in fulfilling the museum's mission and interpretive goals. Including statistics about the number of visitor contacts or staff hours in the training orientation can help provide a sense of worth among trainees. Research shows that visitors tend to learn more and be more satisfied with their experience when trained staff are present to help facilitate interactions. (Marino and Koke, 2003) Discuss how the museum's primary functions—education, research, marketing, PR, security, maintenance, etc.—are affected by interpretation. Think about the various ways your institution would be different without interpreters and share those thoughts with trainees.

4) IDENTIFY THE THEME AND MESSAGES FOR COLLECTIONS, EXHIBITS, AND PROGRAMS

As defined in this manual, the theme is the overriding story or, as Beverly Serrell describes in her book *Exhibit Labels: An Interpretive Approach* (1996), the "big idea" you want visitors to take away with them. The theme should unify or drive all the elements of an interpretive program or interaction. Messages are the supporting evidence—stories, ideas, concepts—that help illustrate the theme. Limiting the number of messages (three is a good target number) discourages interpreters from diluting interpretation with unnecessary facts.

Ideally, the process of creating a theme and supporting messages should be a collaborative effort among the educator, curator, and other staff members. However, since every institution's structure is different, there is no guarantee that such a collaboration of content and audience experts will occur. Trainers might discover that the museum's existing themes neither clearly outline what the visitor is to learn or experience, nor reflect the qualities of successful themes and messages (as outlined in worksheet 1E). In such situations, the trainer may have to work with the appropriate staff to create a theme and messages that effectively focus the institution's interpretive programming efforts.

Themes and messages provide focus for both visitor and interpreter. They ensure that the most important ideas are communicated to visitors with consistency, identify what is most important for the visitor to know, and limit the amount of information interpreters can share with the public. Concepts that are relevant to visitors' lives make interpretation more powerful and real to the visitor.

Creating the theme and messages for interpretation is like writing a five-paragraph essay for an introductory writing class. The introduction includes the *thesis statement,* the overriding premise of your argument, which is equivalent to the theme. The next three paragraphs are the supporting evidence—the facts, ideas, stories, and other research that support the thesis statement—and are equivalent to the messages. The last paragraph is the conclusion, which reviews all the supporting evidence that reinforces the thesis statement. Interpretation without themes and messages is like a road trip without a destination; it may have interesting moments, but you never really get anywhere.

The Collection/Exhibit Facts Inventory (worksheet 1B) is designed to help trainers gather support material from curators, education and exhibits staff, local experts, and even volunteers who have special knowledge of or experience with the collection and/or exhibit. Asking several people to complete the worksheet will add to and diversify the information and perspectives you collect. The ideal would be to use worksheet 1B before an exhibit opens, but is also useful for an existing show. When reviewing the worksheet comments, look for interesting and recurring ideas that might be relevant to visitors, and use those insights to create or revise the theme and messages for interpretive programming purposes. The checklist on worksheet 1E can be used to evaluate new or existing themes and messages to ensure their effectiveness. Exercise 1C and worksheet 1D will help trainers identify themes and messages for their collections, exhibits, and programs. Sample themes and messages are included on pages 15 and 16.

REFERENCES

Marino, Margie, and Koke, Judy. 2003. "Face to Face: Examining Educational Staff's Impact on Visitors." *Dimensions: The Journal of Association of Science and Technology Centers.* January/February.

Complete the following questions:

A. Who are you? (name/type of institution)

B. What do you do? (function of institution)

C. For whom do you do it? (audience)

D. Why do you do it? (institutional goals)

E. How do you do it? (avenues for serving audience and fulfilling institutional goals)

Turn the above information into a statement about your institution by completing the following statement:

It is the mission of (your museum) to (what you do) so that (for whom you do it) may (why you do it) through (how you do it).

Sample:

It is the mission of (A) Blank Gardens (B) to display the hardiest plants growing in the Portland area (C) for local residents and visitors (D) to increase awareness, appreciation, and conversation about plants (E) through research, collections, conservation, and interactive education.

Collection/Exhibit Facts Inventory

Worksheet 1B

> **Collection/Exhibit:**
>
> **Contributor/Staff:**

Note: Designed to be used with projects still in development, this worksheet also can be used with existing collections and exhibits.

General Knowledge

What is your favorite aspect of this collection/exhibit? For example, the one thing you want visitors to know about/see is. . . .

Where is the greatest visitor interest likely to be (and why)?

What stories (folklore, historical tales, potential visitor and staff memories, etc.) are best told here, and where should they be told?

What questions are visitors likely to ask about this collection/exhibit?

What do you think the public's perception (or misperception) of this collection/exhibit might be?

What are the challenges for interpretation in this collection/exhibit (accessibility/narrow paths, temperature, sounds, etc.)?

Historical Significance

What (if any) is the historical significance of this collection/exhibit (highlights, unique pieces)?

Plans for the Future

How will this collection/exhibit change over time?

What long-term plans will influence this collection/exhibit's future?

Object/Plant/Animal	To whom does it appeal?	Why? (rarity, form, story, etc.)

Objects & Display

What was the inspiration for or motivation behind the design of this collection/exhibit? What impression do you hope it will make on the visitor?

Which objects (or plants, animals, etc.) are the "main attractions" for both you and the average visitor? Which objects do visitors ask about the most? Why?

What special care, preparation, or maintenance does this collection/exhibit require, both in storage and while it is on display?

Behind-the-scenes

Which special or behind-the-scenes operating systems, staff, or resources help you install and/or maintain this collection/exhibit?

Resources

If someone wanted to learn more about this collection/exhibit, what resources should they pursue? Please list favorite books, other museums, experts in the field, Web sites, classes, etc.

Theme and Message Development

Exercise 1C

Instructions

The theme and messages identify what is most important for the visitor to know and also limit the amount of information that is communicated. Providing limits helps make the interpretation more powerful and relevant to the visitor.

Creating the theme and messages of your interpretation is like writing a five-paragraph essay. The introduction includes the thesis statement, the overriding premise of your argument, which is equivalent to the theme. The next three paragraphs are the supporting evidence—the facts, ideas, stories, and other research that support the thesis statement—and are equivalent to the messages. The last paragraph is the conclusion, which reviews all the supporting evidence to reinforce the thesis statement.

1) What concepts or topics should be addressed through the interpretation of this location?

   a) Brainstorm about the concepts that are of interest in the collection/exhibit; these usually are one-word ideas (e.g., diversity, oppression, textiles, expression).

   b) Review the list and choose the most important learning concepts. Ask "what do we want the visitor to know about this subject?" and then use "what do we think the visitor wants to know?" to make the interpretation relevant and engaging.

   c) Record these Program Topics on worksheet 1D, Identifying Theme and Messages (page 13).

2) What overriding idea or theme do you want to communicate?

   a) Identify one strong idea from the list to develop into the theme; you can review the list or include other ideas in a supporting message later.

   b) Draft a theme by determining the most important idea the visitor should take away. Review Qualities of a Successful Theme on page 14.

   c) Record this idea under the definition of theme on worksheet 1D.

3) What information supports this idea or could serve as messages?

   a) Brainstorm about several possible ideas. Some of the ideas that were discussed as possible themes might better serve as supporting information.

   b) Review Qualities of an Effective Message (page 14) to ensure that each idea reinforces or clarifies the theme.

   c) Record the three ideas under the definition of messages on worksheet 1D.

Program Topics are the important ideas and story elements (usually a single word) that determine the most important overriding idea—the theme.

Important topics that the visitor should understand, learn, or be exposed to include:

_____

_____

_____

The **theme** is the overriding idea that the visitor should take away from the interpretive experience. The theme summarizes or unifies important program topics and tells the visitor what to expect. It is the plot in your story or thesis statement.

If there were one thing about this collection/topic that I want the visitor to remember, it would be:

_____

_____

This is your theme.

Messages illustrate the theme through supporting evidence, such as stories, experiences, or concepts. Identifying the messages (sometimes called learning points) helps provide focus and limits excessive information that can dilute the interpretation.

I want the visitor to know that:

1. _____
2. _____
3. _____

These are your messages.

Adapted from Environmental Interpretation (1992), page 37, with permission from the author, Sam H. Ham

Qualities of Successful Themes and Messages

Worksheet 1E

Qualities of a Successful Theme:

- ☐ Answers the question "so what?" or "what is worth exploring here?"

- ☐ Grabs attention by posing a challenge, confronting a myth, provoking thought, and/or having universal appeal.

- ☐ More than a single word or idea, but can usually be communicated in one sentence.

- ☐ Written in clear and familiar language that's easy for people (interpreters and visitors) to remember.

- ☐ Focuses attention on memorable/significant aspect of collection/exhibit.

- ☐ Addresses important information, feelings, behaviors, or values related to topic.

- ☐ Interpreter would be satisfied if visitor used this theme to answer the question, "What do you think this program/exhibit was about?"

Qualities of an Effective Message:

- ☐ Written in a familiar language/tone.

- ☐ Relates the theme to visitor's life; makes real and meaningful connections.

- ☐ Reveals facts and meanings by drawing attention to supporting (and sometimes surprising) evidence.

- ☐ Illustrates complex ideas by making analogies or comparisons with known (universal) concepts and objects.

Collection: Butterfly Haven

Theme: Despite its small size, there are complex communities of native plants and insects inhabiting the Butterfly Haven.

Messages:

1) There is a strong interrelationship between butterflies and plants.

2) Adaptations allow the butterfly to survive within its habitat.

3) Observation is the key to appreciating the natural world within the Haven and nature.

Dialogue samples

Questions, props, and actions helps initiate conversations about the messages.

Question and Answer:

Why do you think flowers have brightly colored petals?

Flowers are nature's best advertisers. Petals help attract attention so their pollinators can find their nectar reward in exchange for helping the flower to reproduce. [related to message 1]

Prop and Action:

Use a party horn and blow it to gain visitor's attention.

This horn is very similar in form to a butterfly's proboscis or mouth. Butterflies use their mouths in much the same way we use a straw. We use a straw to drink out of glasses or containers; why do you think the butterfly's mouth is shaped this way? [related to message 2]

Adapted with permission from the Peggy Notebaert Nature Museum of the Chicago Academy of Sciences

Theme and Message with Dialogue Development

Sample 1G

Collection: Evergreen Cemetery

Theme: Evergreen Cemetery holds the secrets, struggles, and survival stories of Santa Cruz Pioneers.

Messages:

1) Each person buried here has stories that connect us to the way of life and everyday struggles in early Santa Cruz.

2) These pioneers may have had diverse backgrounds, but most shared a common dream of starting a new life in California.

3) By preserving Evergreen Cemetery, we are ensuring that the lives and efforts of our ancestors and the spirit of the American pioneer will never be forgotten.

Dialogue samples

Questions, props, and actions helps initiate conversations about the messages.

Question and Answer:

Why do you think this pioneer risked his and his family's lives to come to California?
California was a destination for many families who were looking for a better life. Hopes of "striking it rich" during the Gold Rush encouraged people to make the cross-country trip in a covered wagon, even though they knew it was dangerous. [related to messages 1 and 2]

Prop and Action:

Take a piece of paper and crayon and complete a rubbing of the surface of a gravestone.
This rubbing is more than a reproduction of the words and image on this gravestone; it serves as a reminder of the lives and personalities that shaped Santa Cruz. [related to message 3]

Adapted with permission from the Santa Cruz Museum of Art and History

CHAPTER 2 • # Take Inventory: Identifying Audience, Programs, and Content

In addition to knowing "who" the institution is and where it is going, trainers also must answer another key planning question: "What resources will help us get there?" This chapter will help trainers devise strategies for assessing and using the museum's resources to complement the interpretive framework developed in chapter 1. The first step is to take inventory of the resources at your museum.

IDENTIFY YOUR CURRENT AND TARGET AUDIENCE(S)

Understanding your audience is key to interpretive program development and helps you focus training on how interpreters can anticipate and meet visitor needs. Formal and informal research can identify both the people who already come to your interpretive efforts and the people you'd like to see there. This information will shape the content and style of the training program.

Before embarking on any audience research or data collection, determine the goals of those efforts:

- *What do you want to know, and how will the information be used?* What will result in better programming and train interpreters more effectively? There is no reason to collect information that is not useful or won't be applied by anyone in the institution.

- *What is your time frame, and what are your resources?* Do you have time to develop and administer a formal survey, or do you need help from volunteers, visitor services staff, etc.? Make realistic choices about how much time and money can be invested in this process.

- *How will you collect information?* There are several ways, requiring varying amounts of time or effort, to seek information about your audience. Remember: any effort to understand and train your interpreters to serve your audience is time well spent.

Steps for identifying current audiences include:

1. Collect the existing research:

- Identify whether any market research has been done at your museum. If the institution has membership, marketing, public relations, or grant writing staff, for whom audience information is critical, check with those individuals first.

- Find out from senior management and veteran staff members whether outside studies were conducted at the museum in the past.

- Contact nearby institutions—both those that are similar to yours and those that are different—and ask for information about their visitors.

2. Survey your audience:

- Admissions/information desk representatives or volunteers stationed at the museum's entrance can collect generalized data on ages, ethnicity, and group size of visitors—just by observing the people coming through the doors. Knowing these details can help staff adjust their interpretation to meet visitor needs (e.g., learning how to say "hello" in the languages of predominant visitor groups). Although such informal surveys don't represent a fully scientific process, they can collect basic information without being invasive.

- Visitors also can be asked to participate in a brief survey to "help you better serve their needs." Museums sometimes use an incentive, such as a small gift or admission discount, to encourage visitors to answer questions about who they are, where they're from, why they visit, and how often they come to the museum (see pages 22-23 for a sample visitor survey).

- Formal surveys (written and verbal) can be time-consuming and costly, but the resulting information is invaluable. Carefully designed and administered studies enhance the quality of the visitor response and thus allow for greater application of the findings. Each institution, however, must determine which approach will be of greatest use. For more information on formal surveys and evaluations, see *Practical Evaluation Guide: Tools for Museums and Other Informal Educational Settings* (Diamond, 1999) and *Visitor Surveys: A User's Manual* (Korn and Sowd, 1990).

INVENTORY/ASSESS CURRENT PROGRAMS

Conducting an inventory and assessing the value of current interpretive programs or learning opportunities—based on their success and relevance to the mission and the museum's definition of interpretation (discussed in chapter 1)—helps identify which interpretive efforts to continue, eliminate, or revise.

Worksheet 2B, Interpretive Program Inventory and Assessment, guides the trainer through this process. Once the worksheet is completed, the "effort/reward relationship" of programming will become more evident. In other words, if reaching the right audience with the right messages in an efficient way (the reward) does not outweigh the time and costs invested in creating or maintaining the program (the effort), then you should question the program's viability. Here are some questions that can help analyze the data you've gathered on worksheet 2B and determine the value of each program:

- Do the theme and/or messages of the program need to be developed or revised?

- Are the programs mission-based? Does each one relate to a collection/exhibit and, if so, is it a priority collection/exhibit?

- Does each program incorporate the same interpretive technique, or are there a variety of methods to appeal to diverse learning styles?

- How do program cost and staff time compare to the number of visitors served and the (presumed) quality of their experience?

- Is the museum obligated to retain certain programs to fulfill a grant, serve a target audience, or continue a partnership, regardless of the effort/reward relationship?

- Which programs are most popular with interpreters and visitors? If you could only train interpreters on a few programs, which would they be?

- Which programs have been documented in an easily accessible format to help new interpreters learn and deliver them effectively? (See Elements of Effective Program Write-Ups, page 156.)

If a program needs revision, has low attendance, or costs more than it brings in, consider eliminating that program (at least until it can be revised) from the training workshop, and ask trainees to focus on programs that provide a high reward for their time and efforts. Training should focus on the most successful or important interpretive programs. If there are many successful programs, focus on a few of the most important or popular ones (limiting the number of programs to three helps to keep the session focused).

SOLICIT AND INTEGRATE COLLECTIONS CONTENT

While this manual emphasizes the "process" or techniques of interpretation, it is important to recognize that, like many visitors, trainees want and need the factual content about the collections. The Collection/Exhibit Facts Inventory Worksheet, used in chapter 1 to develop program themes and messages, also can inform trainees about valuable collections- or exhibit-based content. Soliciting the input of curators or other content experts ensures there will be a diverse and relevant foundation of information to support interpretation. In addition, inviting curators or other guest lecturers to make presentations can relieve the trainer from the responsibility of serving as the content expert. Videos, publications, reference lists, and other resources also will supplement and enhance the trainee's knowledge of the site and collection/exhibit.

Some sites may choose to create fact-based training tools, such as conversational scripts or videos of exemplary interpreters. These tools must reinforce the importance of how interpreters can incorporate the interesting content into a *dialogue* with visitors and formulate effective questions to spark a conversation on a particular subject. Questions and conversations should be geared towards communicating the theme and/or message determined for the collection or program.

The following is an excerpt from a conversational script that shows how factual information, as well as the theme and message it aims to support, can be included in a learning dialogue:

> **Theme:** Despite the Butterfly Haven's small size, it is inhabited by complex communities of native plants and insects.
>
> **Message 1:** There is a strong *interrelationship* between the butterflies of the Butterfly Haven and native Chicago plants.
>
> *How are these butterflies similar or different from those you've seen in your neighborhood?* While you may not recognize all these butterflies, each one in the Butterfly House is native to Illinois.
>
> *What do you think it means when researchers say that a certain plant or animal is native?* Generally, a species is considered native when it has lived in a geographic place since before the settlement of European-American people. The plants and animals in the Butterfly Haven have come to depend on each other as natives to the ecosystem of the Chicago area.
>
> *Is anyone here picky about the food they eat?* Most types of the butterfly larvae you see here will only eat only one type of plant. It's similar to the way that most humans primarily drink milk as newborn babies. The caterpillar's food choice is called the larval food plant or host. Many native species are quite fussy about their hosts and need the plants that are only found in our prairies and woodlands.

Trainers can create hypothetical interactions that use questions and actions to model message-based conversations. (For additional examples, see www.visitordialogue.com.)

INTERPRETER MATERIALS

When developing and gathering materials for training, it is helpful to combine all the materials for interpreters in one resource, such as a training binder. However, avoid the "big black binder syndrome" that cripples many museum training programs, which often insist on giving trainees comprehensive information about the collections. Instead, the materials included in the binder should be equally balanced between interpretation techniques (process of learning) and collection/exhibit information (content of learning). This means including only a few key articles or resources as background information.

It is unnecessary (and even detrimental) to give each trainee a copy of every article ever published relating to the content of your collections or exhibits. However, that does not mean that such articles are not valuable. Supplemental learning resources should be made available separately in a series of reference binders or a reference library (with books, magazines, videos, etc.), or presented during enrichment training that fosters ongoing learning in all interpreters. Trainers should be sensitive to the fact that interpreters have a sincere desire for information about content, even as they remind trainees that how that information is delivered is just as valuable. A sample table of contents for a training binder can be found on pages 26-27.

Portland Classical Chinese Garden Visitor Survey

Sample 2A

Purpose: This evaluation is designed to gain feedback from visitors about meaningful Garden experiences, to learn more about who they are, if they are residents of or visitors to Portland, and how the museum can create better learning opportunities for them based on age, gender, and ethnicity.

Instructions:

1. Approach the visitor and ask if she would participate in a brief, five-minute survey to help the Classical Chinese Garden better serve its visitors.

2. Remind her that honest responses will provide the greatest help to the Garden.

3. Let her know that you will begin by getting her feedback about her experience at the Garden and then ask a few general questions for statistical purposes.

Evaluator_____ Date_____ Time:_____

Survey Questions

1. How did you hear about the Garden? (Check all that apply)

   ☐ newspaper article   ☐ tourism information
   ☐ from a friend   ☐ Internet
   ☐ at another garden   ☐ from a Garden volunteer
   ☐ T.V. commercial   ☐ presentation at my organization
   ☐ radio ad
   ☐ other_____

2. What brought you to the Garden today? (Check all that apply)

   ☐ a Garden event   ☐ gift shop
   ☐ came with out-of-town   ☐ guests just curious
   ☐ teahouse   ☐ plants/gardening interest
   ☐ personal enjoyment_____
   ☐ other_____

3. On a scale of 1 to 10, how much do you feel your understanding and appreciation of Chinese culture has increased after your visit(s) to the Garden? (Circle one)

   (1)——(2)——(3)——(4)——(5)——(6)——(7)——(8)——(9)——(10)
   Not at all   Somewhat   Significantly

4. Do you have suggestions for how we could we increase the understanding and appreciation of Chinese culture for other visitors? What information should we offer?

5. In the future, would you be willing to pay $2, in addition to the admission fee, for:
- ☐ a self-guided audio tour about the plants, architecture, and culture of China
- ☐ a plant guide
- ☐ landscaping (stone and water) guide
- ☐ an inscription guide (characters/poetry in the Garden)
- ☐ an architecture guide
- ☐ Are there other subjects you would like more information about?

6. What was the most memorable aspect of your trip today? What did you like most and why?

7. What was surprising about your visit to the Garden? How was it different from what you expected?

8. Do you have any unanswered questions about what you saw/experienced at the Garden? (Was there anything that might be confusing for another visitor?)

9. What do you think of when you hear the following words? What do they mean to you?

Landscape _____

Harmony _____

10. To attract new visitors, what should we tell them about the Garden? What could we do to attract them?

11. Are there any other comments you would like to share?

Gender: Male____   Female____   Home zip code _____
First-time visitor____   Repeat visitor____   Are you a member?   Yes____ No____
Age Range: 1-12   13-17   18-25   26-39   40-59   60-75   76+

Used with permission from the Portland Classical Chinese Garden

Interpretive Program Inventory and Assessment

Program name	Interpretive Technique	Theme/main messages (big idea/learning objectives summarized)	Collection focus/mission-based program?	Who is served? (audience)	# served/ impact (high/low)

Worksheet 2B

Visitors will know, feel, do...	Partners, sponsors, or funding specifications (dates of commitment, evidence of completion)	Cost/Visitor	Visitor comments and/or program challenges	Overall program quality (1 high- 5 low)
K: F: D:				
K: F: D:				
K: F: D:				
K: F: D:				
K: F: D:				
K: F: D:				
K: F: D:				
K: F: D:				
K: F: D:				

Training Manual Table of Contents

Sample 2C

"Oregon History A-Z"
History Guides of the Oregon Historical Society

Training Manual Table of Contents

Section 1: About the Oregon Historical Society
- Oregon Historical Society Mission and Goals
- General Contact Information
- Exhibit Information
- Oregon Historical Society Institutional Timeline
- Strategic Plan, 1999-2004 (values, vision, mission, strategic initiatives)
- Department of Education Mission Statement and Goals

Section 2: Policies and Procedures
- Oregon Historical Society Policies
- Visitor Guidelines
- Visitor Information
- School Group Visits to the Oregon Historical Society

Section 3: Volunteer Information
- History Guides Volunteer Job Description
- Volunteer and Intern Handbook
- Evaluation Goals
- Interpreter Self-Evaluation

Section 4: Interpretation Overview—Worksheets & Research
- Definitions of Interpretation and Artifacts
- Identifying Audiences Needs and Understanding Learning Theory
- Assessing your Resources
- Exploring Interpretive Techniques
- Conversation as Interpretation

Related Articles and Resources
- "Designing Your Exhibits: Seven Ways to Look at an Artifact."
- "The Meaning of Objects."
- "50 Ways to Look at a Big Mac Box."
- "Interpreting Material Culture: A Five-Step Approach"
- "Five Steps to Interpret Material Culture"
- U.S. National Archives & Records Administration: Artifact Analysis Worksheet

Exhibit Specific Content

Section 5: Featured Exhibit Introduction: "Oregon History A-Z"
- Overview of Major Theme and Messages
- Background Information from the Curator

Section 6: Exhibit Floor Plan and Text
- Exhibit Floor Plan (with location of each casual interpretation station for guides)
- "Oregon History A-Z" Label Text
  Introductory Panel
  Archaeological Artifacts
  Bottles
  Chairs
  Scales
  Weather Predicting Goat
  Wheelbarrows
  "Oregon History A-Z" Themes

Section 7: Casual Interpretation Stations—Sample Conversations
- Station 1: Sample Conversational Script for each message
- Station 2: Sample Conversational Script for each message
- Station 3: Sample Conversational Script for each message

Section 8: Structured Interpretation Program Write-Ups
Exhibit Tours
- History Detectives: Grades K-3
- Our Place in History: Grades 4-6
- Stories of the artifacts: Grade 7-8
- Artifacts of the Past and Present: Grades 9-12

Classroom Programs
- History Detectives: Grades K-3
- Our Place in History: Grades 4-6
- Stories of the Artifacts: Grade 7-8
- Artifacts of the Past and Present: Grades 9-12

Section 9: Exhibit-Related Printed Materials
- Gallery Guide for Visitors
- Teachers' Guide

Section 10: Resources
- Suggested Readings on Oregon History
- Suggested Readings on Visitor-Centered Interpretation

Adapted with permission from the Oregon Historical Society

CHAPTER 3 • # The Ultimate Interpreter:
Creating Expectations and Standards

This chapter describes how three components—clear expectations, empowerment, and standards for evaluation—help with the recruitment, training, and retention of interpreters. Establishing expectations and standards supports ongoing review of interpreter performance and ensures that quality interpretation takes place; those discussed here can be applied to both paid and volunteer interpreters.

CREATE EXPECTATIONS WITH JOB DESCRIPTIONS

Job descriptions help staff understand their roles and establish expectations that make managing, evaluating, and rewarding interpreters easier and more effective. The description should include responsibilities of the position, qualifications and training requirements, reporting structure, time and schedule commitment, evaluation expectations, and how interpreters are empowered to improve a visitor's experience (e.g., offer free admission).

Even if your institution does not provide job descriptions for volunteers, you should still outline expectations for volunteer interpreters, which demonstrates the mutual commitment between the museum and its volunteers. See, for example, the Denver Art Museum's Document of Understanding, which outlines expectations of performance for both interpreter and institution (page 33).

Sample descriptions for staff and volunteer interpreters can be found on pages 31 and 32.

DETERMINE METHODS OF EMPOWERMENT

As front-line staff, interpreters are often in a position to "make or break" a visitor's experience. Conversations with visitor services staff, security personnel, and site administrators can reveal how much authority interpreters have to rectify a problem or improve a situation. Trainers should work with the appropriate staff to determine approved methods interpreters can use to solve a visitor's problem; these methods then should be referenced, either in job descriptions or in a separate document. Overhead 10I on page 95 provides examples of empowerment strategies, which help interpreters shape positive experiences and ensure that visitors are treated well. Review this list to determine which strategies your interpreters are authorized to use, based on the institution's policies.

SELECT AN INTERPRETER EVALUATION TOOL

Trainers should establish a system of evaluation that outlines measurable objectives for interpreter performance. Criteria for both self-evaluation and external evaluation (i.e., completed by supervisor, coach, peer, audience, etc.) can set performance standards and provide interpreters with motivation for improving their skills. Trainers also can use evaluation to learn how to improve training and give greater support to trainees. For example, if all the trainees are struggling over how to initiate conversations with visitors, the trainer should not assume that students will never meet that expectation. Rather, it's possible that more training and support are needed. (See also the Workshop Evaluation Form in chapter 4.)

Trainees should understand that evaluation can help improve both the interpreter's skills and the skills of those who train and support them. A sample self-evaluation tool is on page 35, and examples of external evaluations (to be completed by a supervisor, mentor, or the interpreter's peer) are on pages 36 to 39. Use these samples as a model for creating a site-specific evaluation that measures the qualities and performances essential to your museum. For more examples of evaluation tools, see *Great Tours! Thematic Tours and Guide Training for Historic Sites*. (Levy, Lloyd, and Schreiber, 2001)

Position Description:

The interpreter primarily creates and implements interpretive programming for the visiting public, including schools, families, children, and adults. The interpreter will provide both structured interpretive programs and casual interpretative experiences for these audiences.

Reports to:

Manager of interpretive programs

Essential Responsibilities and Skills:
- Presents educational floor programs to museum visitors. Interpretive roles include, but are not limited to: exhibit programming, outdoor tours, storytelling, casual interpretation in galleries, and other seasonal programs.
- Helps develop new program opportunities and staff, volunteer, and programming resource materials, as assigned.
- Helps with general interpretive programming and event support (research, writing, etc.)
- Participates in special education events, such as volunteer training, public festivals, educator previews, and teacher-in-service programs.
- Helps train and coach volunteer interpreters.
- Supports the ongoing functions of the Education Department.

Expectations:
- 40-hour work week.
- Tuesday–Saturday work schedule, with occasional evening or weekend schedules
- Willing to participate in ongoing evaluation program.
- Strives to ensure a positive visitor experience. In particular, listens to visitor comments/complaints, records them on appropriate form, and works to correct any problems by contacting a manager for further interaction, offering free admission passes for future visits, or, in consultation with a manager, reimbursing the admission fee.

Knowledge/Skills Requirements:
- Knowledge of general plant science and ecology.
- Comfortable with public speaking.
- Ability to present science content clearly and share enthusiasm with diverse population of learners.
- Ability to handle multiple projects and tasks at once.
- Organizational and project management skills needed.

Physical Requirements and Availability:
- Ability to carry program supplies to and from presentation areas.
- Ability to lead activities indoors and outdoors.
- Seven-day availability

Minimum Education Required:
- Bachelor's degree in science, education, or related field.

Minimum Experience Required:
- One year of experience teaching in a non-formal setting (museum, zoo, nature preserve).

Volunteer Interpreter Job Description

Sample 3B

Position Description:
- Facilitate conversations and activities for the general public that promote a deeper understanding of the educational goals for each exhibit.

Reports to:
- Manager of interpretive programs

Essential Responsibilities and Skills:
- Staffs indoor and outdoor exhibit areas as needed to engage the public in conversation and scripted activities, using necessary supplies and equipment.
- Guides the visitor experience to ensure a memorable and positive visit; this includes ensuring comfort and safety of visitors while fostering educational growth.
- Works with staff to set-up and breakdown equipment and activities.
- Assists with special educational activities and programs.
- Serves as the liaison between staff and visitor, notifying appropriate personnel about problems or successes in the exhibit area.

Expectations
- Able to work with a team; is enthusiastic, dependable, and flexible.
- Enjoys interacting with the public and communicate effectively with individuals, families, and school groups.
- Willing to learn new information through hands-on experience.
- Comfortable with public speaking.
- Able to react quickly to solve problems or contact a staff person, as appropriate.
- Capable of four hours of physical activity and transporting supplies.

Training:
- Attends general volunteer orientation and additional volunteer interpreter certification training; ideally, one session per quarter.
- Attendance at advanced training opportunities is strongly encouraged.

Schedule Details:
- Arrive at Volunteer office by 9:30 a.m. (morning volunteers) or 1:00 p.m. (afternoon volunteers) for check-in and meeting.
- To help direct visitors, review the list of visiting groups and events occurring at the beginning of your shift.

Commitment:
- Once a week for the weekday shift: 9:30 a.m.–1:30 p.m. or 1:00 p.m.–5:00 p.m.; evening hours also available on Wednesdays. During summer hours (Memorial Day to Labor Day), we ask afternoon volunteers to stay until 6 p.m.
- Every other weekend, either Saturday or Sunday shift: 9:30 a.m.–1:30 p.m. or 1:00 p.m.–5 p.m.
- If you cannot make it to the museum, before the start of your shift notify the Volunteer Department, 888-888-8888.

The Denver Art Museum Provisional Docent Training Program
Document of Understanding
2003-2004

The activities listed below are to be undertaken in the context of the 2003 vision statement for the Education Council:

> A Denver Art Museum docent will make every possible effort to enhance visitors' joy of looking. The docent will recognize each visitor's individuality and enable discovery of a personal connection with the art and an experience of the wonder of human creativity.

As a provisional docent, the volunteer agrees that for 2003-2004:

- To be prompt and reliable in attending training. Two excused absences are permitted.
- To notify a provisional docent liaison if unable to attend training as scheduled.
- To carry out training activities assigned by the Head of School Programs (coordinating this training program) in good spirit, and to seek learning assistance from the staff and experienced docents in situations requiring such guidance.
- To become thoroughly familiar with the museum policies, philosophy and procedures, both written and verbal.
- To pay a materials fee for participation in the provisional docent program ($50 payable on Sept. 8, 2003, and $50 on Jan. 5, 2004).
- To commit to effective communications with socially, economically, culturally, and philosophically diverse audiences.
- To begin giving Enchanted Castle (grades K through 2) and Perception Games (grades 3 through 6) tours early in 2004.
- To begin giving Choice Tours for adults in summer 2004.
- To participate in 2 mornings of AM at the DAM.
- To participate serving family audiences during schools holidays and at weekend festivals in the museum. Minimum number of hours required in 2003-2004 is 6 hours.
- To participate in whatever evaluation program exists, to be open to having staff or experienced docents observe your work in order to offer suggestions for improvement.
- To complete all assignments in a timely manner.
- To accept the museum's right to refuse to invite a provisional docent to be a docent-in-good-standing after proper review by the Dean of Education and the Chairman of the Education Council.
- After completion of provisional docent training, to commit to 2 years as a member of the Education Council which consists of giving a chosen ___ day a week for touring and another ___ day a week for ongoing training, research and attendance at required meetings as well as a maximum of 18 hours of school holiday and weekend time.
- To maintain Denver Art Museum membership in order to be well informed about current activities. *(continues on next page)*

Volunteer Interpreter Document of Understanding

Sample 3C

The Denver Art Museum agrees:

- To provide a written description of the training the provisional docent is to undergo and advance schedule of training sessions.
- To train provisional docents on a level that will permit them to begin their work with students, families, and adults.
- To create certain benefits, including notification of special educational events, educational outings, and social gatherings.
- To provide each person completing the training with a certificate of achievement.

Signed by:

_____   _____

Co-Dean of Education   Date   Provisional Docent   Date

_____

Head of School Programs   Date

Copyright 2004, the Denver Art Museum. Reprinted with permission.

Name   Date

Program/Gallery

Interpretive Technique:

Please rate your response to the following statements.

4 = Never   3 = Sometimes   2 = Most of the time   1 = Always

Before the beginning of my program/shift:

4   3   2   1   I go over the program's theme and messages to focus my interactions.

4   3   2   1   I review universal concepts and potential misperceptions of content.

4   3   2   1   I review the sample questions created to engage visitors.

4   3   2   1   I adjust interpretation content and style for audience (children, adults, etc.)

During my program/shift:

4   3   2   1   I greet visitors and gather information about their previous knowledge.

4   3   2   1   I let visitors know what to expect and give permission to ask questions.

4   3   2   1   I encourage participation and tap visitor knowledge with questions.

4   3   2   1   I include information that reinforces the theme.

4   3   2   1   I listen to visitor questions/remarks and incorporate them into interactions.

4   3   2   1   I relate interpretation to the visitors' lives (make it real, meaningful, etc.).

4   3   2   1   I express my enthusiasm/passion for the subject and the museum.

4   3   2   1   I provide information in a narrative style, rather than just a series of facts.

4   3   2   1   I help visitors to discover something new, rather than just point it out.

4   3   2   1   I encourage visitors to use two or more of their senses.

4   3   2   1   I regularly use props and exhibit elements to engage visitors.

4   3   2   1   I refer visitors to other programs or activities that might be of interest.

4   3   2   1   I thank visitors for coming and invite them to come again soon.

Additional training or research that would help me be more effective in this program or gallery:

My strengths as an interpreter are:

1.

2.

Two things I can improve by the next time I offer this program or work in this gallery:

1.

2.

Interpretive Coaching Form

Interpreter: _____ Date: _____ Grade Level: _____

Reviewer: _____ Program: _____

PREPARATION & SET-UP:	Strengths	Areas to Grow	Comments
Arrival 15 minutes prior to program			
Equipment & set-up			
Greeting of group and starting time			
PRESENTATION:			
Voice, volume, rate, inflection			
Eye contact, facial expression			
Body language			
AWARENESS OF AUDIENCE:			
Rapport			
Vocabulary & information level			
Concern for comfort and safety			
TEACHING TECHNIQUES:			
Explanations & directions			
Questioning skills			
Group management & discipline			
Involvement of participants			
Use of props & equipment			
Pacing, transitions, flow			
Development of appropriate theme			
GOALS & OBJECTIVES MET:			
Opening & introduction			
Keeping focused on theme			
Familiarity with material			
Closing & summary			

Observation Checklist

Person Observed: _____ Date: _____

Observer: _____

Program: _____ Grade/General Age of Group: _____

Please use a separate piece of paper to record your answers.

1. Pay attention to the introduction. What are the elements of a good introduction? Did the guide do anything different from what you do? If so, what? Did you think the introduction was effective? Please comment.

2. What types of questions does the guide use? Are the majority "yes/no," "fill-in-the-blank," or "open-ended"? Give an example of an open-ended question (one that has no right or wrong answer).

3. How does the guide use his/her voice? Spend several minutes listening. How many kinds of inflections were used? Did he/she vary the volume? What seemed to be effective? Please comment.

4. In what ways does the guide make eye contact? Is eye contact used to control the group or an individual or while waiting for an answer? Explain.

5. Listen for silences. Does the guide talk constantly or are there periods of quiet? Give examples.

6. What seems to be the main emphasis of the program—the imparting of knowledge or the experience itself? Is there a combination of both? Explain.

7. Does the group seem comfortable with the guide? Is there rapport? Are the visitors active participants or merely observers?

8. Does the guide use humor in the program? Is it effective?

9. Circle your choices: The guide spoke too fast, too slowly, or just right. The program was hurried or paced appropriately. The walking speed was too fast, too slow, or appropriate for the interest and age of the group.

10. Which activities and/or visuals were used? Were they an integral part of the program or were they used as a filler?

11. What can you apply to your own presentation?

Adapted from Spring Valley Nature Center, Schaumburg Park District, Schaumburg, Ill.

External Evaluation

Sample 3F

Evaluation Instrument

Date/time of day: _____   Crowd (circle one):   light   medium   heavy

Guide's name: _____   Evaluator's name: _____

Station: _____   Amount of time observed: _____

Ratings:

n/a = not applicable; 0 = unsatisfactory; 1 = needs improvement; 2 = did okay; 3 = did well

Skills Rating:	n/a	0	1	2	3	Comments:
Was appropriately dressed	n/a	0	1	2	3	
Looked receptive, ready to talk	n/a	0	1	2	3	
Was friendly and positive	n/a	0	1	2	3	
Faced audience while talking	n/a	0	1	2	3	
Stood so audience could see exhibit(s)	n/a	0	1	2	3	
Had theme or focus	n/a	0	1	2	3	
Spoke loudly enough	n/a	0	1	2	3	
Spoke clearly	n/a	0	1	2	3	
Used hands to direct attention	n/a	0	1	2	3	
Modeled appropriate behavior	n/a	0	1	2	3	
Used props appropriately	n/a	0	1	2	3	
Gave accurate information	n/a	0	1	2	3	
Used suitable vocabulary	n/a	0	1	2	3	
Used appropriate anecdotes	n/a	0	1	2	3	
Related information to visitors' lives	n/a	0	1	2	3	
Encouraged participation with open-ended questions	n/a	0	1	2	3	
Listened to questions and remarks	n/a	0	1	2	3	
Credited questions	n/a	0	1	2	3	
Encouraged use of two or more senses	n/a	0	1	2	3	
Solved problems gently and effectively	n/a	0	1	2	3	
Closed talk by directing audience to exhibit(s) of interest	n/a	0	1	2	3	

Guide's Strengths:

_____

_____

_____

Guide's Weaknesses:

_____

_____

_____

Suggestions for improvement made by the evaluator:

_____

_____

_____

Suggestions for improvement made by the guide:

_____

_____

_____

Overall Rating of Guide's Performance:

| Excellent | Very Good | Good | Fair | Poor |

Recommendations:

_____ Re-evaluate in _____ month(s)

_____ Retraining (specify) _____

_____ Other (specify)_____

Guide's Signature: _____Date: _____

Evaluator's Signature: _____Date: _____

Developed by Chris Parsons while at the Monterey Bay Aquarium.

CHAPTER 4 • # Make a Plan: The Logistics of Success

This chapter outlines the steps for placing the icing on the "training cake." Once all the other tasks have been completed, the finishing touches can provide clarity and structure for training sessions and participant feedback. To ensure the interpretive training runs smoothly, the trainer should complete the following five tasks:

1) SELECT A TRAINING FORMAT

The training format should reflect the desired interaction between interpreters and visitors. Constructivist learning, inquiry-based learning, and cooperative learning, for example, are different types of educational methodologies that encourage conversation and interaction. Trainers should select the methodology most appropriate for their interpretive style.

Constructivist interpretation determines the learner's existing knowledge and then introduces new concepts and information using hands-on activities. Relating new ideas to everyday examples (i.e., making it real and meaningful) solidifies the visitor's understanding.

Cooperative learning utilizes small-group, hands-on exercises to reinforce concepts and ensure that everyone in a group participates in learning. This method of learning relates directly to the visitor-interpreter interaction. Some of the exercises can be converted to mini-programs, which the interpreter can use to engage the visitor.

Inquiry-based learning is infused in the methodologies listed above and is based on the Socratic method of teaching. Students process thoughts by answering questions and reiterating information in their own words, which helps them grasp the concepts and ideas being communicated.

These are just a few approaches that can inform and guide a training program. The exercises in this manual emphasize these techniques, but readers certainly can incorporate other perspectives. For more information and background on learning techniques, see the resources listed in chapter 18.

2) FIND A TRAINING SPACE

The training space should foster an interactive, team environment (i.e., it should be something other than an auditorium with fixed seating) and allow direct access to the collection, exhibit, or designated setting for practicing interpretation techniques. Ensuring in advance that you have the correct A/V equipment will help the training run smoothly. In addition, you'll need to secure break-out rooms, consider how to facilitate movement between the training locations and the collection/exhibit, and develop strategies (e.g., colored stickers on name tags) for breaking trainees into small groups during training exercises.

3) CREATE THE TRAINING GOALS AND OUTLINE

Goals will keep both trainer and trainees focused and on schedule. Typically, each training session has several goals; some may be content-based while others may focus on process outcomes for the group. Some examples of training goals include:
- to provide a basic introduction to interpretation and its role at the museum
- to incorporate theory that suggests that conversation and social interaction are where museum learning occurs
- to provide hands-on opportunities that allow trainees to apply learned techniques
- to reinforce the importance of knowing both content and interpretive techniques
- to foster ongoing growth in interpretive skills and knowledge
- to offer team opportunities for professional and skills development
- to strengthen a sense of team among interpreters

An outline that gives a structure and schedule (including time for breaks and group activities) helps keep trainers on task, creates expectations for trainees, and generates momentum.

4) PREPARE A TRAINING EVALUATION FORM

To ensure that the training is effective in promoting conversations among visitors, ask trainees to evaluate the session. Evaluation provides a wonderful opportunity to see how to enhance the training and strengthen the trainer's skills. The sample training evaluation form on page 44 can help you create a site-specific evaluation tool for your museum. Give careful consideration to your training goals and be certain to solicit feedback about whether those goals were met.

5) COMPLETE THE TRAINING PREPARATION WORKSHEET

Worksheet 4B allows trainers to review and check off the tasks outlined in chapters 1 through 4. The final step is to combine all the materials developed for the training into a central reference that can serve as a part of the institutional memory.

Interpretive Training Evaluation

Sample 4A

Offered by: _____ Date: _____

Please rate your response to the following statements:

1 = Strongly Agree   2 =Agree   3 = Disagree   4 = Strongly Disagree

1) This training met my expectations based on the goals stated at the outset of the session.

    1   2   3   4   *Comments:*_____

2) This workshop demonstrated the benefits of interactive interpretation and modeled learning through the use of dialogue.

    1   2   3   4   *Comments:*_____

3) This training offered adequate opportunities to apply what I've learned in the museum.

    1   2   3   4   *Comments:*_____

4) The information presented in this workshop will enhance my interpretation at the museum.

    1   2   3   4   *Comments:*_____

5) The printed materials reinforced the concepts being taught.

    1   2   3   4   *Comments:*_____

6) The trainer effectively facilitated discussion/learning on this subject.

    1   2   3   4   *Comments:*_____

7) After completing this training, I feel prepared and confident about engaging museum visitors in learning conversations.

    1   2   3   4   *Comments:*_____

8) My favorite part of this training was:

9) If I could change something about this training for future participants, it would be:

10) If I could have more training, it would focus on:

11) Is there anything else you want the trainer (or management) to know about your experience with this training?

My primary function at the museum is_____:

    ☐ Interpreter (front-line)   ☐ Education: your role:_____

    ☐ Visitor Services   ☐ Management/administration of _____

    ☐ Other_____

I participated in: (please check all that apply)

    ☐ **Module 1:** Overview of Interpretation

    ☐ **Module 2:** Interpretive Opportunities

    ☐ **Module 3:** Developing New Interpretive Programs

Mission:

Your definition of **Interpretation:**

Current/Target **Audience(s):**

Checklist

☐ Each collection/exhibit and interpretive program has established **themes** and **messages.**

☐ **Interpretive Program Inventory** has been completed and priority programs selected.

☐ Selected programs are available in accessible format (program write-ups) for the interpreter's future use.

☐ **Content** experts and resource materials are available for the training session.

☐ Carefully selected resources (programs, conversational scripts, institutional information, etc.) have been combined in accessible **training binder for trainees.**

☐ **Job descriptions** have been created for each interpreter in the training session.

☐ **Methods of empowerment** have been discussed and approved by the museum's administration and appear in interpreter's job description.

☐ Appropriate **evaluation tool(s)** have been selected and created for interpreters.

☐ **Training format** is based on and designed to follow desired learning model(s).

☐ Appropriate **space and logistic** needs have been considered to ensure a quality experience.

☐ **Training goals and outline** reflect the workshop's logistics and format.

☐ A **training evaluation form** has been developed to improve future training.

☐ All materials listed above have been collected to create **central reference (binder) for future trainers.**

Notes:

Module 1 Training Outline: An Interpretive Overview

Four-Hour Training Session

Key:

Questions for trainees

👁 Overhead

( ) Interactive Exercise

◿ Worksheet

Training Tools Used in Module 1 (in the order in which they appear).

- Learning through Conversation 5A

    👁 The Evolution of Interpretation (definitions) 6A

    👁 The Benefits of Conversational Interpretation 6B

    ( ) Skits: the Principles of Interpretation 6D (trainers), 6E (trainees)

    👁 Freeman Tilden's Principles of Interpretation 6C

    👁 The A.R.T. of Interpretation 6F

    ( ) The Role of the Interpreter Exercise 7A

    👁 Steps of Visitor Involvement 7B

    ( ) Tangible, Intangible, and Universal Connections 7C

    👁 The A.R.T. of Interpretation 6F

    👁 Maslow's Hierarchy of Needs 8A

    👁 How Do People Learn? 8B

    👁 Conversation in the Museum? 8C

    👁 Making Play Educational 8D

    ( ) Assessing Our Resources exercise 9A

    👁 Resource Survey 9B

    ◿ Resource Survey 9C

    👁 Forms of Personal Interpretation 10A

    👁 Guidelines for Successful Interpretive Technique 10B, 10C

    ( ) Objects as Stimuli to Learning Conversations 10D

    👁 Objects as Stimuli to Learning Conversations 10E

    ( ) The Difficult Visitor 10F

    👁 Identifying Difficult Visitors 10G

    ◿ Identifying Difficult Visitors 10H

    👁 Methods of Empowerment 10I

    👁 Implementing Conversation 10J

    👁 Why Conversation? 10K

Module 1 Training Outline: An Interpretive Overview

Four-Hour Training Session (cont.)

Training Introduction: Chapter 5
- Explain to trainees how the training day will be structured and how their basic needs will be met in terms of bathroom breaks, food, rest breaks, etc.
- Introduce the idea of conversation as the premise of interpretive training.
    - 👁 Learning through Conversation 5A
- Review goals of Module 1:

    Provide foundation for importance and role of interpretation in the museum.

    Provide model for conversational interaction desired on between interpreter and visitor.
- Add other goals developed by trainer in chapter 4.

Elements of Successful Interpretation: An Overview: Chapter 6

A. UNDERSTANDING INTERPRETATION
- *What is interpretation?*
- *What do you think of when I say "interpretation"?*
- *What might other people think when they hear the word?*
    - 👁 The Evolution of Interpretation 6A (definitions)
- *How does this definition of interpretation differ from the way interpretation has been traditionally employed at our institution?*

Ask trainees to think of their own experiences at museums. Emphasize conversation and guided interaction.

B. THE BENEFITS OF CONVERSATIONAL INTERPRETATION
- *How do we benefit from interpretation at our sites?*
    - 👁 The Benefits of Conversational Interpretation 6B

C. THE PRINCIPLES OF GOOD INTERPRETATION
- *Given what you now know of interpretation, who in your life has served as an interpreter (helped you to understand something new)? For example, parents, teachers, religious and political leaders, etc.*
- *Why were they successful?*
- *Let's see if those reasons are reflected in Freeman Tilden's principles.*
    - ( ) Skits: The Principles of Interpretation 6D (trainers), 6E (trainees)
    - 👁 Freeman Tilden's Principles of Interpretation 6C

Principles incorporated into the A.R.T. of Interpretation
    - 👁 The A.R.T. of Interpretation 6F
- *Why is it important to know our **audience**?* (solicit general responses)
- *What should you know about the **resource** or site?*
- *How does **technique** influence the interpretive experience?*

Careful consideration of the A.R.T. of Interpretation provides more opportunities for interpretation to occur. We'll revisit A.R.T. later in the training.

D. QUICK REVIEW

What is the purpose of interpretation and what are some ways museums benefit from it?

Making Connections: The Role of the Interpreter: Chapter 7

A. THE ROLE OF THE INTERPRETER

Now that we've reviewed the elements of interpretation, we need to understand the role the interpreter plays in making it happen.

   ( ) The Role of the Interpreter Exercise 7A

   • *Why does the museum exist?* (record all answers on flip chart)

   • *Why do people visit your museum?*

Interpreters are the bridge between the reason the museum exists and the reason people come. Interpreters connect the messages of the site to the real and meaningful world of the visitor.

   • *Why does it matter if we connect our visitors to our site?*

      ◉ Steps of Visitor Involvement 7B

   • *What kinds of experiences cause a visitor to move up the steps of involvement?*

B. FACILITATING THE CONNECTIONS

Review the definition of interpretation, i.e., any communication that enriches the visitor experience by connecting the value of the institution's messages and collections to the real and meaningful world of the visitor. This exercise demonstrates one way to initiate those connections:

( ) Tangible, Intangible, and Universal Concepts Exercise 7C

   • *What do you interpret here?* (record tangible and intangible concepts on two separate charts)

   • *Describe how this object looks, feels, smells, how it might taste. (tangible /intellectual)*

   • *How does it make you feel or what does it remind you of? (intangible/emotional)*

To appeal both to the real (factual) and meaningful (emotional) world of the visitor, good interpretation must include both tangible and intangible elements.

   • *Which elements are universal—i.e., something everyone can relate to—and why is that important?*

Referencing family, change, money, death, reward, childhood makes interpretation relevant and meaningful to the greatest number of visitors. (Circle items on the flip charts that are universal.)

Tangible, intangible, and universal concepts connect visitors to the site; they are valuable tools for successful interpretation. But every aspect of the A.R.T. of Interpretation—Audience, Resources, and Techniques—is important.

Refer briefly to this overhead to provide structure for subsequent discussions:

👁 The A.R.T. of Interpretation 6F

Introducing Trainees to the Audience: Chapter 8

A. Understanding the Audience

Audience is the "A" in the A.R.T. of Interpretation.

- *What do you know about the people who visit your site? (Who are they?)*
- *Who are they and what do we know about why they visit?*

Regardless of who they are, all visitors have some basic needs.

👁 Maslow's Hierarchy of Needs 8A

B. The Way People Learn

- What helps people to retain knowledge?

👁 How Do People Learn? 8B

How does what we know about the way people learn support the idea of conversation as interpretation?

👁 Conversation in the Museum 8C

- *Do you remember Tilden's principle about children? Children and adults have different learning needs.*

👁 Making Play Educational 8D

Investigating the Museum: Chapter 9

A. Evaluating the Available Resources

The second aspect of the A.R.T. of Interpretation involves an assessment of your resources.

( ) Assessing Our Resources Exercise 9A

- *How do we learn about/research our museum and the content of its collections?*

List non-personal and personal resources on flip charts.

B. Why We Collect Information about the Museum

👁 Resource Survey 9B

Explain each question included in the survey.

✎ Resource Inventory 9C

Trainees should complete the worksheet individually or in small groups, preferably within the museum and in consultation with other staff/interpreters. This also could be a homework assignment.

Exploring Interpretive Techniques: Chapter 10

A. PERSONAL INTERPRETATION

Choosing the appropriate technique comes after understanding the audience and resources.

- *Which interpretive techniques are used at this site?*
    - 👁 Forms of Personal Interpretation 10A

While some tips for interaction may be intuitive, it is always good to review:

- 👁 Guidelines for Successful Interpretive Technique 10B and 10C
- () Objects as Stimuli to Learning Conversations 10D
- 👁 Objects as Stimuli to Learning Conversations 10E

B. DEALING WITH DIFFICULT VISITORS

- () The Difficult Visitor 10F
- 👁 Identifying Difficult Visitors 10G

List examples of each obstacle and ask trainees to identify strategies to overcome them.

- 📝 Identifying Difficult Visitors 10H
- 👁 Methods of Empowerment 10I

C. QUICK WRAP-UP

End on a supportive and upbeat note, focusing on the benefits of conversational interpretation.

- 👁 Implementing Conversation 10J

It's more than talking. . . .

- 👁 Why Conversation? 10K

Module 1 Training Outline: An Interpretive Overview

Two-Hour Training Session

To shorten the training session, several group activities have been eliminated and worksheets that can be assigned as homework have been highlighted.

Key:

Questions for trainees

👁 Overhead

( ) Interactive Exercise

✐ Worksheet

Training Tools Used in Module 1 (in the order in which they appear).

- Learning through Conversation 5A
    - 👁 The Evolution of Interpretation (definitions) 6A
    - 👁 The Benefits of Conversational Interpretation 6B
    - 👁 Freeman Tilden's Principles of Interpretation 6C
    - 👁 The A.R.T. of Interpretation 6F
    - ( ) The Role of the Interpreter Exercise 7A
    - 👁 Steps of Visitor Involvement 7B
    - ( ) Tangible, Intangible, and Universal Concepts 7C
    - 👁 The A.R.T. of Interpretation 6F
    - 👁 Maslow's Hierarchy of Needs 8A
    - 👁 How Do People Learn? 8B
    - 👁 Conversation in the Museum? 8C
    - 👁 Making Play Educational 8D
    - ( ) Assessing Our Resources exercise 9A
    - 👁 Resource Survey 9B
    - ✐ Resource Survey 9C (assign as homework)
    - 👁 Forms of Personal Interpretation 10A
    - 👁 Guidelines for Successful Interpretive Technique 10B-C
    - 👁 Identifying Difficult Visitors 10G
    - ✐ Identifying Difficult Visitors 10H (assign as homework)
    - 👁 Methods of Empowerment 10I
    - 👁 Implementing Conversation 10J
    - 👁 Why Conversation? 10K

[T]he range of experiences [in a museum] often requires rethinking the roles of staff and volunteers. In essence staff become facilitators rather than disseminators of information, supporting learning rather than directing it.

Lynn D. Dierking, et al. • "The Family and Free Choice Learning" • Museum News (2001)

CHAPTER 5 • # Introduction to Interpretive Training

Module 1 provides an overview of interpretation, highlights its value to the institution, and explains the museum's expectations regarding interpretive efforts to both new and current volunteers. Most museums will offer this module to each new training group and ask veterans to attend a refresher session—perhaps an abbreviated version in conjunction with a topical guest lecture—once a year. Veterans can attend this training as mentors for an incoming class of volunteers, which will allow them to add their experience to the group exercises and discussion while also creating early bonds between new and current interpreters.

Depending on the museum's training schedule, Module 1 can take place in a single afternoon or be broken up into several two-hour sessions. Trainers can shorten the schedule, if necessary, by condensing some of the small-group, break-out sessions into a larger group discussion and asking trainees to complete worksheet exercises as homework. The outline offered on pages 47-51 is designed to take place over four hours, with ample time for small-group work and activities. For suggestions on how to create a two-hour training session, see page 52.

The workshop's introduction sets the tone for the training and outlines the interpreter's role in accomplishing departmental objectives and fulfilling the institution's mission. Through simple interactive exercises, it also explains the training goals (defined in chapter 4) and how interpreters (or other staff) will be able to apply the lessons learned in the future.

At this point, trainees may benefit from a review of the interpreter's job description created in chapter 3. Reviewing the expectations for interpreters will remind trainees that they will be held accountable for using information and skills learned during the training exercises. In addition, providing scheduling and organizational details up front minimizes questions or concerns and frees participants to focus on the content.

During the introduction, the trainer should:
- welcome trainees
- introduce herself and any other trainers (if applicable) and define their ongoing involvement with interpreters
- discuss schedule and/or plan for training; review agenda (include mention of breaks and bathroom locations)
- summarize training goals
- introduce concept of conversational interpretation
- generate excitement about the value of conversation as a training process and explain that this progressive style of interpretation is based on current visitor studies
- if appropriate, go over Learning through Conversation (overhead 5A) to underscore that conversation will be the training method used
- invite trainees to introduce themselves; ask them to share something about themselves and their relationship to this institution or museums in general (e.g., why they decided to become interpreters, their favorite or most memorable experience interacting with a visitor, etc.)
- explain (or ask the group to generate a list identifying) what trainees should expect from the trainer—good listener, responsive to questions, willing to interact with trainees, etc.
- explain (or ask the group to generate a list identifying) what the trainer should expect from trainees: to give their best efforts, ask for clarification if needed, review of their job descriptions and reporting structures, and evaluate the workshop
- review the museum or department's mission and discuss interpreters' role in fulfilling that mission
- respond to questions from trainees about schedule, expectations, etc.
- facilitate an "icebreaker" activity to set an interactive tone for the workshop

". . . the purpose of conversation [in the museum] is to help visitors construct a richer personal understanding of the collections and its effect on their lives and communities."

—*Phil Parfitt, 1998*

[Successful museum programs] have conversational flavor— even if no words are spoken. These conversations have content focus—even if they are not part of an obvious lesson. There is the assumption that the visitor is not some poor soul in need of enlightenment, but a smart and capable collaborator.

—Michael Spock, "Elegant Programs and Conversations,"
Presence of Mind: Museums and the Spirit of Learning, 1999

Constructivism builds upon the learner's existing knowledge and adds new information that she can relate to through hands-on/ minds-on experience.

Cooperative learning maximizes group learning by facilitating an exchange of ideas between learners.

Inquiry-based learning is infused in the ideas listed above and is based on the Socratic method of teaching. Students process thoughts by answering questions and reiterating information in their own words, which helps them grasp the concepts and ideas being communicated.

Our learning is intimately associated with our connection
with other human beings, our teachers, our peers,
our family, as well as casual acquaintances, including
the people . . . next to us at the exhibit. . . .

George Hein • "The Museum and the Needs of People" (1991)

CHAPTER 6 • # The Elements of Successful Interpretation: An Overview

This chapter summarizes the history of interpretation and explains the importance of making interpretation real, meaningful, and compelling to visitors. Trainees first will review the various definitions of interpretation, which will provide opportunities to discuss the history of the profession and also clarify what that history means to the museum.

The field of interpretation is relatively new, with its first major publications issued in 1920, *Adventures of a Nature Guide and Essays in Interpretation* by Enos Mills, and 1957, *Interpreting Our Heritage* by Freeman Tilden. Mills wrote about his experiences as a nature guide and offered insights on how others could become more effective guides. "The aim is to illustrate and reveal the alluring world outdoors," he wrote, and was the first to refer to a guide as an interpreter or someone who translates unknown information into something more understandable.

Tilden studied the interaction between National Park Service (NPS) rangers and visitors to the parks. He not only created a definition for the field, but identified six principles inherent in successful interpretation (see overhead 6C). Although there have been significant contributions to the field since Tilden's 1957 book, his definition of interpretation was used widely until 1996, when NPS issued its definition: "Interpretation facilitates a connection between the interests of the visitor and the meanings of the resource." In 2000, the National Association for Interpretation expanded the NPS definition to address the importance of making both intellectual and emotional connections with the visitor. In recent years, the museum community also has begun to evaluate the impact of interpreters and conversation on informal learning and meaning-making, influenced by current educational theory that suggests that authentic learning occurs when learners are invited to share their own knowledge and experiences. (Thier, 1976; Moll, 1990; Hein, 1995; Falk and Dierking, 2000; Leinhardt et al., 2002; Marino and Koke, 2003) As visitor studies specialists Deborah Perry and Kris Morrissey note, "Learning in a museum is the meaning that we create as we engage in communication with one another—communication about who we are, our place in the cultural and natural world, and our relationship to the things and people around us." (Perry and Morrissey, 2002)

Interpreters who are trained to use brief, message-based, and personalized conversations, rather than "canned" or non-personalized programs, are more likely to address the visitor's intellectual and emotional needs. The Evolution of Interpretation (overhead 6A) provides a focal point for a trainee discussion on how to personalize interpretation; the importance of knowing the evolution of interpretation; why visitor experiences and conversation are a central part of informal learning; and how the benefits of social interaction can be realized in every type of museum. When discussing the definition of interpretation included in this book, point out two things:

- Conversation does not always have to be between two or more people; it also can refer to an internal thought process or development of ideas.
- The phrase "guided interaction" suggests that interpretation should provide visitors with the tools they need to interact with exhibits and programs. It should give the visitor "new eyes" or instruction on how they and their companions can have a more meaningful museum experience. For example, interpretive programs and labels should offer suggestions for how to interact with the collection, such as, for example: "Touch the object in front of you. What does the surface remind you of?"

To further the discussion on conversation, present The Benefits of Conversational Interpretation (overhead 6B). Ask the group to consider the relevance of this list by taking each "benefit" and explaining how it might be applied in the museum. For example, for "Increases Visibility," some museums have created a tour, exhibit, or a sign to draw attention to a location or issue of high importance to the institution.

Trainers then can launch a discussion of the elements of successful interpretation by reviewing Tilden's "Principles of Interpretation" (overhead 6C) and showing how they might apply to real-life situations. One way to accomplish this is in an easy, interactive exercise (see exercises 6D and 6E) during which trainees take on the roles of interpreters and visitors. Trainers may experience some initial resistance to participating in "skits" as a training activity, but trainees should soon come around; this exercise is regularly cited as one of the highlights (mostly for the laughter it generates) of Training Module 1. Regardless of how you choose to present the principles—with or without a skit—you should emphasize their connection to successful interpretation and provide a thorough review of their applications.

The A.R.T. of Interpretation (overhead 6F) introduces three essential aspects of comprehensive planning for effective interpretation—audiences, resources, and techniques. Knowledge of the audience helps interpreters determine how to be effective and sensitive when making connections with various visitor groups. Knowledge of the available resources not only improves the quality of the content, but also involves others in the interpretation process, and thus building ownership. Knowledge of successful and appropriate interpretive techniques allows interpreters to build on their strengths and appeal to diverse audiences. By discussing each component of the A.R.T. of Interpretation, trainees will learn the importance of making information site-specific and applicable in every setting. NPS, for example, emphasizes that interpretation must incorporate "universal meanings"—for example, concepts related to family, change, birth, death, fear, and other common experiences and feelings—and connect in some way to every visitor. (Larsen, 1999)

The A.R.T. of Interpretation is a foundation for Training Module 1. Each component of A.R.T. will be explored more completely in chapters 8, 9, and 10.

Overhead 6A

A nature guide (interpreter) is a naturalist who can guide others to the secrets of nature. It is not necessary for them to be a walking encyclopedia. They arouse interest by dealing in big principles, not with detached and colorless information.

Enos Mills, Adventures of a Nature Guide, 1920

Interpretation is an educational activity which aims to reveal meanings and relationships through the use of original objects, by first hand experience and illustrated media rather than simply to communicate factual information.

Freeman Tilden, Interpreting Our Heritage, 1957

Environmental Interpretation involves translating the technical language of a natural science or related field into terms and ideas that people who aren't scientists can understand.

Sam Ham, Environmental Interpretation, 1992

Interpretation facilitates a connection between the interests of the visitor and the meanings of the resource.

National Park Service, 1996

Interpretation is a communication process that forges emotional and intellectual connections between the interests of an audience and the inherent meanings in the resource.

National Association for Interpretation, 2000

Interpretation is conversation, guided interaction, or any communication that enriches the visitor experience by making meaningful connections between the messages and collections of our institution and the intellectual and emotional world of the visitor.

The Interpreters Training Manual for Museums, 2004

How does your institution define interpretation?

If planned and implemented properly, conversational interpretation can:

> ### ⇥ Attract Visitors

Interpretation is a product that invites and holds visitor interest.

> ### ⇥ Increase Visibility

Interpretation sends the message that there is something worth seeing here.

> ### ⇥ Enhance Recreational Experience

Interpretation engages visitors personally while giving them an opportunity to learn something about what they are seeing.

> ### ⇥ Create a Positive Image

By offering engaging experiences and desired information, the museum sends the message, "We care about our visitors and their needs."

> ### ⇥ Increase Public Understanding and Awareness

Interpretation should reinforce the value of the museum's mission and messages while promoting understanding of the decisions of museum management.

> ### ⇥ Preserve/Protect the Collection/Exhibit

By educating visitors about what is valuable and how their behavior can affect the collection, interpretation serves as a management tool.

> ### ⇥ Encourage Social Interaction and Increase Learning

An interpreter who seeks ways to initiate conversations both during and after the museum visit promotes lasting connections to the institution and ongoing learning.

Overhead 6C

1. **Interpretation that does not relate** to the personality or experience of the visitor **is sterile.**

2. **Interpretation is revelation** based on information.

3. **Interpretation is an art** (and combines many arts).

4. **Interpretation is provocation**, not instruction.

5. **Interpretation should aim to present the whole** rather than a part and should address the whole person rather than any one phase.

6. **Interpretation for children is not a dilution of an adult presentation**; it is a fundamentally different approach.

(Tilden, 1957)

How do these principles apply to real-life conversations in museums?

Need: ☐ **a minimum of 2 volunteers** for each skit. It is best if the entire group has an opportunity to participate in some way, with one person acting as an interpreter and another playing the part of a visitor.

☐ **props** are optional, but they can make the activity more museum-specific.

☐ 6 copies of **exercise 6E**; give one copy—each one with a different principle highlighted—to each group of volunteers.

Goal: To illustrate the principles of effective (and ineffective) interpretation with visitors while creating an informal or playful training atmosphere.

What the Trainees Will Do:

- Training groups are assigned to create a skit that exemplifies one of the principles of interpretation.
- Each group illustrates a poor example and a good example of the principle.
- The entire group discusses the skit to further illustrate the principle.

What the Trainer Should Do:

- Divide the training group into six smaller groups. If this is a very new or young group of interpreters, you may want to ask veteran staff to serve as group leaders.
- Provide each group with an instruction sheet (exercise 6E), and highlight a principle for those trainees to consider.
- Give the groups no more than 10 minutes to prepare their skits and remind them to portray both a poor example (what we don't want) and good example (what we do want) of the principle.
- If any trainees are not participating in the skits, schedule a break or facilitate a discussion about people in their lives that act as interpreters—i.e., people who helped them understand or care about something new, such as teachers, parents, and religious and political figures.
- Once the small groups are ready, invite each group to perform its skit in a random order.
- After the members of each small group performs their skit, ask them to remain in place while the larger group reviews the illustrated principle. Ask the group to identify the skit's effective elements. Discuss ways that the good example could be improved upon; then perhaps ask the small group to perform the skit again, this time incorporating suggestions made by the larger group.
- Thank each small group and encourage applause (or even a candy reward) to acknowledge their participation.

Principles of Interpretation: Skits

Exercise 6E

Instructions for Trainees

A. Consider the experiences you have had as a museum visitor or interpreter.

B. Review the principle you have been assigned (see below) and brainstorm about ways this principle can be illustrated. You may choose to recreate your personal experiences or stick to those you have witnessed. An effective (and entertaining!) approach is to offer a poor example (what we don't want to do) followed by the improved, or good example (what we do want to do).

C. Prepare a brief (approximately five-minute) skit to illustrate both a poor and good example of your principle. Props are not necessary, but encourage audience members to use their imagination.

D. When it is your group's turn to perform the skit, introduce your team members and set the stage by telling the audience where the interaction is taking place and if there are any "imaginary" props.

Freeman Tilden's Principles of Interpretation

1. *Interpretation that does not relate to the personality or experience of the visitor is sterile.* For example, comparing a place where no one has been, such as the extensive sand dunes that lined the lake front in Chicago 1,000 years ago, to a place the visitor has personally experienced, such as the Indiana Sand Dunes.

2. *Interpretation is revelation based on information.* For example, weaving important facts about a subject into an unfolding story; asking visitors questions to help them discover the message.

3. *Interpretation is an art (and combines many arts)*, whether materials presented are scientific, historical, architectural, or otherwise. Any art is to some degree teachable; for example, interpreters often use storytelling, music, costumes, performance, and crafts—coloring, painting, etc.—to make interpretation effective and engaging. Interpreters must assess their personal strengths and use those talents to enhance their interpretation.

4. *Interpretation is provocation, not instruction.* For example, after discussing how an 18th-century landscape has changed since European settlement, an interpreter might ask visitors to consider how it might look 50 years after current restoration efforts, and discuss how they might participate in that restoration.

5. *Interpretation should aim to present the whole rather than a part and should address the whole person rather than any one phase.* For example, interpreters should present the big picture, then focus on the smaller pieces that complete the story, making sure to address both factual and emotional connections and catering to different learning styles through multi-sensory activities.

6. *Interpretation for children is not a dilution of an adult presentation; it is a fundamentally different approach.* For example, use clear, descriptive language; employ their imagination; get down on their physical level; let them help create a story about what they are learning.

A = audiences
Who are they and how do they learn?

R = resources
What personal and non-personal

sources of information are available to

create/support interpretation?

T = techniques
How will you engage your audience?

Socially mediated learning in museums does not only occur within an individual's own social group; powerful socially mediated learning can occur with strangers perceived to be knowledgeable [including] museum explainers, docents, guides, and performers.

John H. Falk and Lynn D. Dierking • Learning from Museums: Visitor Experiences and the Making of Meaning (2000)

CHAPTER 7 • # Making Connections: The Role of the Interpreter

This chapter includes a series of activities to help interpreters connect the value of the museum and its collections and exhibits to the interests of the visitor. Visitors who feel connected to the institution are more likely to support it through repeat visits, registering for classes, membership, volunteering, and sponsorship. Interpretation and those who facilitate it serve as the bridge between the institution's goals and the visitor's interests.

Exercise 7A illustrates the interpreter's role in serving as the bridge of understanding between the institution and the visitor. Trainers should ask the trainees to create two lists, identifying "why the museum exists" and "why visitors come." Encourage them to be honest when listing visitor motivations. Although many visitors seek greater knowledge, some—such as young people in some school groups—may not have come voluntarily. Others may head straight to the café or to see a special event. Although there will be some evident similarities between the two lists, it is important to note that museum goals (such as teaching about the collections) do not always meet with visitor interests (such as going to the gift shop). It is the interpreter's role to be the link between the reasons the museum exists and the reasons visitors come.

Steps of Visitor Involvement (overhead 7B) shows trainees why it is important to create experiences that invite visitors to increase their involvement in and connection to museums. People at step 1 seek a recreational experience; they visit the museum while on vacation, with family and friends, or even to go to the café or gift shop. Such recreational visits can lead to repeat visits and, eventually, these positive experiences may encourage people to see the museum as a refuge (step 2). Some visitors become interested enough to seek more knowledge through classes, lectures, or programs (step 3). However, it is important to acknowledge that many visitors may initiate their involvement with a museum at this third step—to learn more about a particular topic through a class or an exhibit, for example.

Most visitors at step 4 can be described as people who are "connected to the museum," visit regularly, and have some ownership in the institution; they often are inspired to become staff members, volunteers, members, advocates, and patrons. Visitors at step 5 have had such positive experiences, they want to actively support the museum's goals by becoming board members and donors. If the museum creates experiences based on the idea that every visitor may be a future museum supporter, then it increases its potential for survival in the future.

There is evidence that most museum visitors are casual visitors (Falk and Dierking, 1992) seeking recreation and refuge (activities associated with the first two steps of involvement). But where do museums direct much of their non-operations budgets? My experience suggests that funding is largely directed at developing educational classes and lectures, membership benefits, and donor events, which are all activities for visitors seeking knowledge, a connection, or to give their support (those already at steps 3, 4, and 5). In other words, a disproportionate amount of staff and financial resources is spent preaching to the choir rather than on recruiting new choir members. But if more resources were dedicated to serving casual visitors—personalized visitor services, conversational public programs, and inclusive events, etc.—they would be more likely to increase their level of involvement. It is the increased involvement of each visitor—whether she's at step 1 or step 5—that is essential to the museum's survival.

How can interpreters create experiences that encourage greater visitor involvement?

Identifying tangible, intangible, and universal concepts of a place, collection, or person helps visitors make connections to the museum. (Dahlen et al., 1996) Exercises 7B and 7C are adapted from materials created by the National Park Service's Interpretive Development Program and help trainees create experiences that help visitors make those connections. Tangible concepts can be experienced or accepted by most visitors. Examples include descriptors such as color, textures, smells, tastes, sounds, and facts, such as the year the object was created, the materials used to construct it, etc.

Intangible concepts are meanings, associations, memories, etc.; highly influenced by personal experience, they will vary greatly from individual to individual. It is these meanings that help visitors to connect with the subjects. Questions to encourage discussion about an object's intangible nature might include:
- What do you think of when you see this?
- When was the first time you saw something like this?
- What was happening in your life at that point?
- What do the colors remind you of?

Unfortunately, often interpretation stops once the tangible information is presented. Intangibles are equally, if not more important, for making connections with visitors.

Finally, it is worth determining which of the listed tangible and intangible concepts are universal—i.e., able to be understood or experienced by every visitor, regardless of her personal experiences. Typically, universal concepts are related to family, change, birth, death, money, fear, work, and other common experiences and feelings. Referencing the elements that can be identified as universal is a valuable strategy for connecting with everyone in an audience.

REFERENCES

Dahlen, D.; Larsen, D.; Weber, S.; and Fudge, R. 1996. "The Process of Interpretation: Fulfilling the Mission through Interpretive Competencies." *1996 Interpretive Sourcebook: Proceedings of the National Interpreters Workshop*: 106-108.

Falk, John H., and Dierking, Lynn. 1992. *The Museum Experience*. Washington, D.C.: Whalesback Books.

The Role of the Interpreter

Exercise 7A

> **Need:**
>
> ☐ 2 flip charts/markers
>
> ☐ 1 volunteer to write

Goal: To illustrate the critical role that interpreters play in connecting visitors to the museum.

What the trainer needs to do:

Let's review what is known about this site. Why does the museum exist? What did the founders have in mind?

>Solicit answers from the group and record on flip chart 1.

>Examples: research, education, collections, history, entertainment, encourage family learning/interaction, legacy, tourism

Why do people visit?

>Solicit answers from the group and record on flip chart 2.

>Examples: entertaining guests, tourists, special events, gift shop, field trip, restaurant, family outing, day care, air conditioning, bathrooms

Take a minute to find the similarities and differences on each list.

>Comparing two lists should make it clear that although there may be some overlap, the reasons that the museum exists do not always match the reasons visitors visit. How do we address this discrepancy?

>Interpreters are the bridge between the museum and its visitors. They connect the museum's messages to the real and meaningful world of the visitor.

Why does it matter if we connect our visitors to our site?

To survive, the museum must have the support of the public. It can achieve that support by understanding why people visit.

>👁 Steps of Visitor Involvement (overhead 7B)

Give some examples of people who might be at each "step."

What kinds of experiences cause visitors to increase their level of involvement in the museum?

Now, let's proceed to Exercise 7C, which examines how emphasizing tangible, intangible, and universal concepts in interpretation can help visitors connect with the museum.

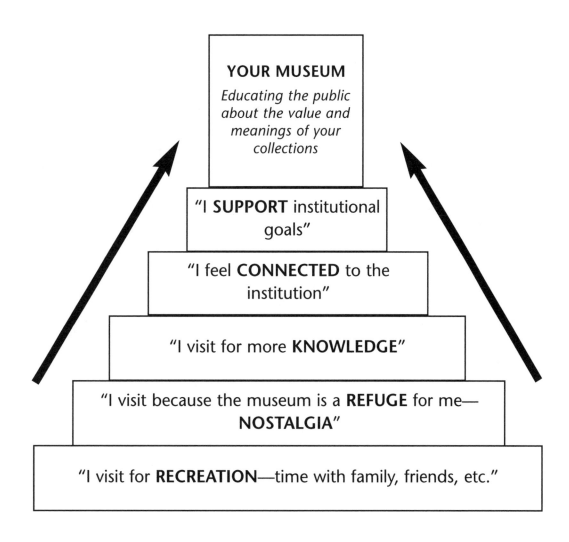

YOUR MUSEUM
Educating the public about the value and meanings of your collections

"I **SUPPORT** institutional goals"

"I feel **CONNECTED** to the institution"

"I visit for more **KNOWLEDGE**"

"I visit because the museum is a **REFUGE** for me— **NOSTALGIA**"

"I visit for **RECREATION**—time with family, friends, etc."

Give some examples of people who might be at each step?

What kinds of experiences cause visitors to move up these steps?

Tangible, Intangible, and Universal Connections

Exercise 7C

Need:

- ☐ 2 flip charts/markers
- ☐ 1-2 volunteers to write
- ☐ 10 similar objects to interpret (for small groups to share)

Note: objects that relate to the museum are preferable, but may not work as well if they are too familiar to the trainees

---

Goal: To **reinforce the definition of interpretation** (see below) and show how references to tangible, intangible, and universal concepts can facilitate meaningful connections.

Interpretation is conversation, guided interaction, or any communication that enriches the visitor experience by making meaningful connections between the messages and collections of our institution and the intellectual and emotional world of the visitor.

What the trainer needs to do:
- Divide trainees into small groups of three to four people.
- Distribute one object to each group.

Describe how this object looks, feels, smells, or even how it might taste. What are other observable or known facts about the people, places, or events linked to this object? (Tangible connections include observable characteristics and known facts.)

1. Ask the groups to spend a few minutes discussing and recording their answers.

2. Ask representatives from each group to share a few observations with the larger group.

3. Ask a volunteer to record the responses that represent tangible concepts on the flip chart.

4. Thank the volunteer and ask her to return to her group.

How does the object make you feel? What does it remind you of? (Intangible connections include meanings, relationships, processes, values, ideas, and beliefs.)

1. Ask the groups to spend a few minutes discussing and recording their answers.

2. Invite a volunteer to record responses that represent intangible concepts on the flip chart.

3. Ask the groups to share and record their observations.

What is the difference between the charts? (tangible versus intangible)
Discuss why both are important.

All successful interpretation can be described as linking a tangible resource to its intangible meanings. Effective interpretation is about connecting one to the other—tangibles and intangibles exist together.—David Larsen, *Meaningful Interpretation* (2003)

Can all tangible and intangible concepts be equally effective at making interpretation relevant to visitors? Why or why not?

Which elements are universal (something to which everyone can relate)?
Circle the elements on the two flip charts that can be considered universal.

Why are universal concepts important in interpretation? Does this object have any other universal qualities?
Universal concepts—such as those relating to family, change, joy, birth, death, money, reward—make interpretation relevant and meaningful to the greatest number of visitors.

Tangible, intangible, and universal concepts enhance the visitor experience by providing a way for people to connect to the museum's messages, collections, and exhibits. This exercise can be applied to every concept or object you interpret.

Adapted from an activity created by the National Park Service (Dahlen et al., 1996)

Asking an interpreter a question should not be like taking a drink from a fire hose.

Freeman Tilden • Interpreting Our Heritage (1957)

CHAPTER 8 • # Introducing Trainees to the Audience

This chapter introduces trainees to how people learn, why they visit museums, and how knowledge about visitors enhances interpretive efforts. Trainers should share the site-specific audience demographics collected in chapter 2 to prepare for the training.

The focus here is on the "A" of the A.R.T. of Interpretation—i.e., the importance of knowing your audience. Ask trainees to describe the museum's audiences, who they are and why they visit, and compare that information to what is known about the institution's target audience. Remind them that even if we know who our visitors are, we still must understand their individual needs, their ability to learn, and how interpreters can help them connect with the museum.

In his 1954 book *Motivation and Personality,* which practitioners still cite today, Abraham Maslow described what he called a Hierarchy of Needs—i.e., the circumstances that effect human motivation. He believed that actualization—loosely defined as striving to reach one's fullest potential—was the driving force of human development. But he also felt people could not strive to reach their potential if certain needs, such as safety, shelter, etc., were not met. Maslow divided his Hierarchy of Needs into basic needs, intermediate needs, and growth needs.

In the same way, museums cannot expect their visitors to be eager to learn about the collection/exhibit if their basic needs have not been met (see overhead 8A). If a visitor in search of a bathroom approaches an interpreter, she doesn't want a lecture on fossils. To use a real-life example, students from one urban school found it hard to concentrate on the virtues of a botanical garden, saying they were afraid that the squirrels were rats with fluffy tails. An interpreter's first task is to ensure that the visitor's physiological and safety needs have been addressed; otherwise she won't be open, as Maslow would say, to pursuing actualization, i.e., learning something new. Only then should the interpreter focus on the visitor's intermediate needs, such as learning about new places or concepts, gaining understanding for previously unknown objects, or appreciating an object's aesthetics.

Overhead 8B, a continuum that illustrates how people learn, is based on Edgar Dale's Cone of Learning (1969) and the work of current educational psychologists who believe that learning is enhanced with both verbal and visual information. (Clark and Paivio, 1991) According to these experts, people tend to remember more of what they say and do rather than information they simply hear, say, in a lecture-style presentation—evidence of the value of conversational interpretation and guided interaction. Overhead 8C lists a few quotes that show how museum-based audience evaluation professionals support the role conversation plays in museum learning experiences.

Providing opportunities to "do" or to participate in learning helps visitors of all ages. Incorporating "play" into learning activities both engages children and gives permission to adult visitors to do the same. Overhead 8D explains how to make "play" an educational activity, especially with children. As Tilden's sixth principle of interpretation (see chapter 6) states, activities for children should be fundamentally different, more than just a dilution of an adult presentation. But the practical examples in overhead 8D, originally written as suggestions for facilitating interaction with children, also work with adult learners of all ages.

To get the conversation started, ask the trainees how the element of play applies to adult learners.

REFERENCES

Clark, J. M., and Paivio, A. 1991. "Dual Coding Theory and Education." *Educational Psychology Review* 3 (3), 149-170.

Dale, Edgar. 1969. *Audio-Visual Methods in Teaching*. New York: Dryden Press.

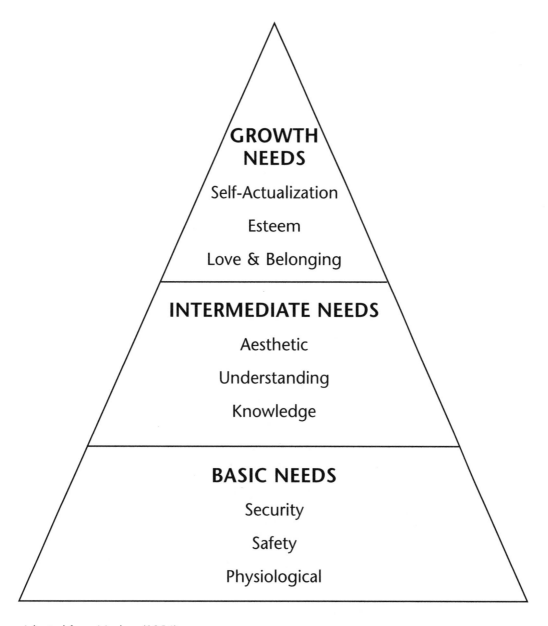

GROWTH
NEEDS

Self-Actualization

Esteem

Love & Belonging

INTERMEDIATE NEEDS

Aesthetic

Understanding

Knowledge

BASIC NEEDS

Security

Safety

Physiological

Adapted from Maslow (1954)

A Continuum of Learning

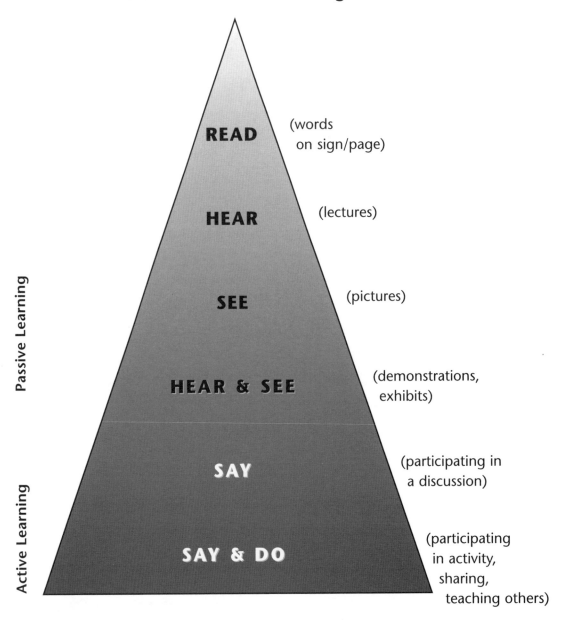

How does this reinforce the premise of learning through conversation and guided interaction?

Learning in a museum is primarily a social process;
people learn through interaction with peers. . . .
Educators do not impart information as much as
provide appropriate means of access to cultures of
science, history, art, and other subjects.

George Hein and Mary Alexander in
Museums: Places of Learning (1998)

**Learning in a museum is the meaning we create
as we engage in communication with each other**:
communication about who we are, our place in the
cultural and natural world, and relationship to the
things and people around us.

Deborah Perry and Kris Morrissey in
Designing for Conversation (2002)

Capitalize on children's natural-born **leadership skills.**

Employ their senses; get them actively involved in learning.

Encourage parents to be involved; give them a role.

Model the desired behavior—sharing, listening, respecting.

Pique children's curiosity; ask their opinions and thoughts.

Use a **language they understand**—colors, size, shapes.

Compare and contrast the new object/idea to familiar ones.

Encourage the use of **descriptive words.**

Ensure **equal involvement** with roles or responsibilities.

Illustrate ideas with short stories, props, or music.

Recognize positive behavior with verbal praise.

Get down to the **child's physical level.**

Don't hesitate to answer a question with **"I don't know."**

Give permission to be playful, imaginative, even goofy.

Remember that **each child is different;** use multiple strategies.

CHAPTER 9 • Investigating Museum Resources:
History, Stories, and People

Every museum has unique and compelling stories woven into its collections and institutional history. These stories, the evidence that supports them, and the people who tell them comprise the museum's resources—the "R" in the A.R.T. of Interpretation. Trainers and interpreters alike can access these resources through staff interviews and institutional research. A quick brainstorming activity (exercise 9A) will help trainees list all the resources with information about the institution. These resources include both non-personal sources, such as those found in libraries, archives, and the Internet, and personal sources, such as reports from original research and interviews.

Trainees can use the Resource Survey Worksheet (9C) to conduct their own research about the museum. Each question either reveals a different story about the museum or helps the interpreter feel like a visitor again. This gives trainees more details about the institution while reminding them about the reasons people visit and the visitor's potential perceptions of the museum. Before they complete the Resource Survey, review overhead 9B and discuss the meaning of each question; this will help trainees understand how to focus their efforts as they complete the worksheet.

This also is a good opportunity to review the Collection/Exhibit Facts Inventory trainers asked staff and other experts to complete in preparation for the training (see worksheet 1B). Most interpreters find that collecting information from their museum colleagues not only makes their work more compelling, it also increases interpretation's credibility among the staff. Contributing to the development of the museum's interpretation encourages curators, administrators, and other staff to become invested in its content.

Assessing Our Resources

Exercise 9A

> **Need:**
>
> ☐ 2 flip charts/markers
>
> ☐ 1 volunteer to write on flip chart
>
> ☐ copies of worksheet 9C for all trainees

Goal: To have trainees consider the available resources for researching the museum or a specific gallery, enhancing an interpretive program, or finding an answer to a general question.

The trainer should ask trainees to list:

1. non-personal research sources: where can we find information related to the museum without talking to a staff person?

   Some examples: museum and public libraries, brochures, institutional Web site, newspapers, magazines, documents from another organization, e.g., a historical foundation

2. personal research sources: who can give us insight and information on our role at the museum?

   Some examples: exhibit developers/specialists, veteran employees, volunteers, members, visitors/stakeholders (school groups, teachers, parents/caretakers, other museum professionals)

The following information will provide direction as interpreters conduct primary research to support their work as interpreters.

- 👁 Overhead 9B: Resource Survey
- 🖉 Review worksheet 9C and discuss the reason for each question.
- () If group is large enough, break into small groups. Ask each group to designate a recorder, who will use a blank copy of worksheet 9C to record the group's answers. (This activity also can be completed as an individual exercise.)

Then ask trainees to:

1. Discuss each question on worksheet 9C, in large or small groups as the recorder documents their responses.

2. Group by group, report a few responses for each question

3. Collect all the completed worksheets from the recorders for eventual entry into central resource binder, where they can be reviewed by interpreters. The diversity of responses should serve as a reminder of the museum's diverse audiences.

Name of Museum: Who are we?

Mission: What are we about? Why are we here?

Short Description/History: Where do we come from? When did we open, and why?

What was your first impression of this museum?

Be the visitor! What is it like to visit here? What is your favorite part?

What interests visitors the most? (most popular exhibit, program, experience)

Consider high-traffic areas, frequently asked questions, program attendance, or popular informational pieces (e.g., self-guided materials, take-home brochures, collection fact-sheets, or other promotional information created by the museum). Answer this question: "If visitors only had 30 minutes, what should they see?"

Who is connected to (or invested in) this museum?

Who would miss the museum if it disappeared? For example, community groups, schools, interest groups, researchers, etc.

Based on your observations (visual and aural), what interpretation challenges does this museum face?

Consider accessibility, lack of tangible or real collections, program space.

What is the public perception of this museum (expectations, misunder-standings, etc.)?

Think about information obtained from marketing and advertising promotions and informal visitor/volunteer/community interviews.

Which museums are similar to or associated with this one (due to topic or location)?

Anticipate visitor expectations, connections, potential comparisons, and confusion.

Resource Survey

Worksheet 9C

Name of Museum:

Mission:

Short Description/History:

What was your first impression of this museum?

What interests visitors the most? (most popular exhibit, program, experience)

Who is connected to (or invested in) this museum?

Based on your observations (visual and aural), what interpretation challenges does this museum face?

What is the public perception of this museum (expectations, misunderstandings, etc.)?

What museums are similar to or associated with this one (due to topic or location)?

CHAPTER 10 • # Exploring Interpretive Techniques: Presentation and Intervention

This chapter introduces trainees to various forms of personal interpretation, including tours, demonstrations, characterization, and casual interpretation (overhead 10A). These are valuable tools for creating site-specific interpretation that reflects the skills of the interpreter. While this manual highlights those methods that foster conversations between interpreter and visitor, each of these forms has the potential to be interactive. It is up to interpreters to determine how to engage visitors in a dialogue.

Trainers can begin by asking trainees to review overhead 10A and discuss the opportunities for interaction in each form of interpretation. Trainers also should identify the forms of interpretation conducted at the museum and those that trainees will use. Trainees participating in Training Module 2 (see chapter 12) also will have an opportunity to practice various forms of interpretation and apply interactive elements.

Although many interpreters have had a foundation in public speaking, trainers still should review basic presentation skills and customer service qualities; see Guidelines for Successful Interpretive Technique (overheads 10B and 10C). Ask trainees to explain how they might employ each guideline in their interactions with visitors.

Overheads 10B and 10C both emphasize the importance of using interactive questions and techniques to connect with visitors. (See Training Module 2 for a more in-depth discussion of this topic.) Michigan State University professor Kristine Morrissey developed exercise 10D, which she and Visitor Studies Specialist Deborah Perry use in their workshop "Designing for Conversation." This exercise, "Objects as Stimuli to Learning Conversations," encourages trainees to put themselves in the museum visitors' shoes by evaluating an unusual or a familiar object. To guide this analysis, overhead 10E prompts trainees to consider a series of questions. "What do you know about this object?" helps them to list facts and observable characteristics. "What do you think you know?"

generates various hypotheses based on their observations. "What do you want to know?" helps them determine which unanswered questions or outstanding curiosities still need to be addressed.

At the end of the exercise, trainees will be able to see how objects can spark conversations that facilitate learning. Talking or speculating about something with others not only increases the potential for fun, but also can inspire people to learn about themselves, each other, and the world. In addition, if objects from the museum's collection are used during the training, this exercise can prepare trainees for conversing with visitors or addressing potential questions during an actual interpretive program.

Finally, interpreters are the front-line staff; they represent the face of the institution to the public. This is usually an enjoyable role, but sometimes interpreters must interact with difficult or frustrated visitors. A difficult visitor can negatively affect everyone else's experience. Exercise 10F is a light-hearted method for showing trainees how to identify and deal with difficult visitors. Overhead 10G describes several types of difficult visitors. Trainees can discuss their own experiences during exercise 10F and record recommended methods for dealing with problem visitors on worksheet 10H.

If a visitor approaches an interpreter with a problem or frustration, as the face of the museum, the interpreter must immediately try to correct or improve the situation. Overhead 10I was designed to help interpreters feel empowered when they respond to frustrated visitors. Trainers should ensure that the recommendations in 10J correlate to the methods of empowerment discussed in chapter 3.

At the conclusion to Training Module 1, trainers should remind all trainees—whether volunteers, education or visitor services staff, or concessionaires—why conversation is at the heart of a positive learning experience for visitors. Briefly take a moment to be the cheerleader for this cause and acknowledge the challenges and strategies for implementing conversation (overhead 10I). Overhead 10K features a quote from Phil Parfitt, former vice president of the Chicago Academy of Sciences, which reinforces the powerful role conversation plays in making lasting connections with visitors. It reminds trainees that conversation is about "mutual learning and teaching; it is a whole lot more than talking."

- Interpretive demonstrations or programs
- Tours
- Storytelling
- Characterizations

  first-person interpretation

  third-person interpretation

  mascots

- Casual interpretation
- Music
- Theatrical presentations
- Video and slide shows
- Facilitated feedback after presentation
- Other forms?

In both structured and casual interpretation:

- **Greet and welcome guests:** set the tone, gather information.

- **Grab their attention:** ask a question, use a prop, offer amazing statistics.

- **Create a dialogue:** request visitor input, share perspectives, recognize prior knowledge.

- **Inclusive comments:** build on visitor comments, refer to visitors' names, hometown, etc., during the presentation.

- **Props:** encourage sensory involvement, highlight "the real thing."

- **Project your voice:** enunciate, make sure you can be heard, adjust volume as necessary.

- **Body language:** yours and theirs; consider facial expressions, eye contact, posture, gestures.

- **Humor:** if it comes naturally to you, use humor; but use it wisely and be sensitive and timely.

- **Language:** use words that generate mental pictures, use specifics, watch slang.

- **"I don't know"** should be a comfortable answer to a question but suggest, or offer to find out, where to get the answer.

- **Transitions:** create bridges between ideas, establish comparisons or connections, and link different ideas or objects thematically.

If you have **a captive audience** for the program:

- **Before the program**

    Learn about the visitors.

    Build anticipation by alluding to program highlights.

    Let visitors know what to expect.

- **Introduction**

    Promise that you'll make it worth their effort.

    Introduce the theme and messages.

- **Bridge**

    Answer the unspoken questions: "why was that just said?" and "how does it apply to me?"

    Keep visitors interested and involved by asking questions that get them thinking about the theme.

- **Body**

    Offer messages to support the theme.

    Provide factual support.

    You don't have to offer a linear presentation; ask for visitor questions and about visitor interests to increase relevance.

- **Conclusion**

    Summarize messages.

    Reinforce theme.

    Offer parting thoughts, call to action, and closing cues.

Adapted from Regnier, Gross, and Zimmerman, The Interpreters Guidebook (1994)

Objects as Stimuli to Learning Conversations

Exercise 10D

> **Need:**
>
> ☐ miscellaneous objects (one object for every two to three trainees)
>
> ☐ Overhead 10 E

Goal: To show trainees how objects can stimulate conversation and facilitate learning about themselves, each other, and the world.

What the trainer needs to do:

- Divide trainees into small groups (approximately two to three people per group).
- Distribute the objects, one per group.
- Ask trainees to look at their object carefully and consider the following questions:

    👁 Overhead 10E

    What do you know about the object?

    What do you think you know?

    What do you want to know?

- Ask trainees to record their responses a piece of paper.
- Then present these follow-up questions for discussion:

    What did you learn from looking at the object?

    What did you learn from each other?

    Did you find you knew things that you didn't even realize you knew? Did the conversation help you synthesize your thoughts or reflect on past experiences or knowledge?

- Once discussion is complete, reiterate how talking or speculating about something with others not only increases the potential for fun, but also can inspire people to learn about themselves, each other, and the world.

Adapted with permission from Kris Morrissey, Ph.D., Michigan State University

What do you **know** about this object? (facts, observed characteristics)

What do you **think you know**? (hypotheses based on observations)

What do you **want to know**? (unanswered questions/curiosities)

The Difficult Visitor

Exercise 10F

> **Need:**
>
> ☐ 10 volunteers to provide "difficult visitor" scenarios
>
> ☐ 10 copies of 👁 overhead 10G, one for each volunteer
>
> ☐ enough copies of worksheet 10H for all the trainees

Goal: Identifying and developing strategies to overcome difficult situations with visitors to ensure successful interpretation.

What the trainer needs to do:

- Ask 10 volunteers to think of a situation with a difficult visitor. Referring to overhead 10G, ask each volunteer to focus on a different type of difficult visitor.
- Remind all other trainees that they will create strategies for dealing with these visitors.
- Instruct the volunteers to recall or create a scenario where they dealt with (or can imagine dealing with) their assigned difficult visitor.

  Remind the volunteers that you do not want to hear (yet) how they would or did handle the situation. They will have an opportunity to share when the entire group offers strategies.

- While the volunteers are devising their scenarios, review the list of difficult visitors on 👁 overhead 10G, one at a time. Ask the trainees to discuss the list of qualities that describe each type of difficult visitor. Encourage trainees to record those qualities on 🗒 worksheet 10H.
- Ask volunteers to share their scenarios (in random order), providing some details to set the scene. Details might include:

  a) where the interaction occurred (e.g., in the gallery, in the visitor center)

  b) what was happening at the time of the interaction

  c) who was there (e.g., only interpreter, other visitors, other staff)

- Ask the volunteers to explain why they suspected, perceived, or were told the visitor was being difficult.
- Then ask the group to identify the type of visitor described in the scenario. There may be some overlap in responses; there is no right or wrong answer.
- After each volunteer confirms/reveals the type of visitor she was describing, solicit strategies from the group for handling the situation. Monitor and modify responses based on the museum's policies. Ask trainees to record desired strategies on worksheet 10H.

The Derailer

Takes discussion in different direction, asks unrelated questions

The Detailer

Wants specific details, interrupts for clarification or to ask questions

The Dominator

First to answer questions, initiate participation, makes loud comments

The Distractor

Continually makes loud comments, physical noises/actions, and/or jokes

The Disagreer

Has different information, insists that interpreter is wrong

The Devout Believer

Believes there is only one explanation, is not open to possibilities

The Devil's Advocate

Disagrees for the sake of controversy, likes to "mix it up"

The Dasher

Always rushing, looking at watch, anxious about time commitment

The Disengaged

Avoids eye contact or physical proximity, has side conversations

The Daunting

Gets upset, challenges authority, makes physical or verbal threats

The Derailer

    Qualities:

    Strategies:

The Detailer

    Qualities:

    Strategies:

The Dominator

    Qualities:

    Strategies:

The Distractor

    Qualities:

    Strategies:

The Disagreer

    Qualities:

    Strategies:

The Devout Believer

    Qualities:

    Strategies:

The Devil's Advocate

    Qualities:

    Strategies:

The Dasher

    Qualities:

    Strategies:

The Disengaged

    Qualities:

    Strategies:

The Daunting

    Qualities:

    Strategies:

You are the face of the institution. How you interact with the public can make or break a visitor's experience.

When dealing with a frustrated or disappointed visitor:

1. Ask her to **review** the entire problem. LISTEN!

2. **Empathize!** Don't take her comments personally.

3. **Repeat** her comments and ask for confirmation and/or accuracy.
   Refer the visitor to the proper authority if the problem is beyond your responsibility.

4. **Ask how** she would like to see the situation **resolved.**

5. Tell her **what you can do** and how you plan to **follow-up.**

6. **Offer something** as a gesture of gratitude (for her comments) or consolation (for her trouble). For example:
   - free tickets for another visit or special event
   - refund entire or partial cost of today's visit (parking or admissions)
   - provide discount at café or gift shop
   - offer souvenir (usually best for issues related to children)

7. **Give her options** for voicing her concerns elsewhere (comment box, manager, online).

8. **Thank her for taking the time** to share her concerns; assure her that the museum will learn from this experience, and invite her back (offer free tickets).

Implementing conversation requires:

- **a mind-shift. . .**

  Conversation as interpretation is a new but proven technique; be a leader in the museum field and try it!

- **sharing successes**

  Share positive stories of what has worked with other interpreters.

- **institutional support**

  Content of collections and process of learning are equally valued by the museum.

- **ongoing practice/development**

  Look to staff and other interpreters for ongoing support; everyone is adapting to this new way of promoting learning.

- **confidence**

  Remember, not every visitor will engage, but it is still worth the effort!

Even when visitors don't speak, they learn when they are surrounded by conversation.

. . . when you leave a conversation
you have left a circle of acquaintance . . .
a society with whom you have shared a topic
and something of yourself.

You take away a better understanding
of both the topic and the other people
that were absorbed in it with you. In turn,
you leave something of yourself behind.

Conversation in this way is a social art,
focused on mutual teaching and learning.
It is a whole lot more than "talking."

Phil Parfitt (1999)

Key:

Questions for trainees

👁 Overhead

( ) Interactive Exercise

📝 Worksheet

Training Tools Used in Module 2 (in the order in which they appear).

👁 Characteristics of Structured and Casual Interpretation 11A

👁 Defining Theme and Messages 11B

📝 Collections Survey 11C

📝 Initiating Message-Based Conversations 11D

👁 Qualities of Good Questions 11E

📝 Identifying Questions 11F

📝 Using Questions to Convey Messages 11G

( ) The Chain of Interpretation 11H

( ) Incorporating Conversation Into Existing Interpretive Programs 12A

👁 The Role of Transitions 12B

👁 Qualities of Transitions 12C

📝 Tour Transitions that Reinforce Theme and Messages 12D

( ) Applying Interpretive Techniques to Content Presentations 13A

📝 Applying Interpretive Techniques to Content Presentations 13B

👁 The Value of Evaluation 14A

Training Introduction: Chapter 5 (review)

- Explain to trainees how the training day will be structured and how their basic needs will be met in terms of bathroom breaks, food, rest breaks, etc.

- Reinforce the idea of conversation as the premise of interpretive training

- Review *goals* of Module 2:

   Provide practical tools for initiating learning conversations with visitors.

   Provide opportunity to incorporate interactive techniques into existing interpretive programs.

   Reiterate need to translate factual information related to programs or collection into questions or ideas that relate to visitor's interests.

- Add other goals developed by trainer in chapter 4.

Module 2 Training Outline:
Applying Interactive Techniques to Interpretive Opportunities

Casual Interpretation: Chapter 11

A. CASUAL VERSUS FORMAL INTERPRETATION

- *How many of you have served as interpreters at a museum or similar site?*
- *Has everyone had an experience with an interpreter while visiting a museum?*
- *Think back to those interactions. How many of you casually interacted with an interpreter in a gallery or on-site outside of a scheduled program?*
- *How many of you participated in a more formal program, such as a tour, lecture, or demonstration, that was led by an interpreter?*

Interpreters facilitate learning interactions in both casual and more structured settings. Both are needed if museums want to maximize their potential for reaching visitors.

- *What are some examples of casual interpretation? List on chart 1*
- *How is formal interpretation different from this? List on chart 2*
    - 👁 Characteristics of Structured & Casual Interpretation 11A

B. DISCUSS THEME AND MESSAGES

No matter the location or collection, it is important to clarify your communication goals. Trainers should present and discuss theme and messages they identified for the collection/location in chapter 2. With the group of trainees, identify areas where the messages are represented within the collection.

   👁 Defining Theme and Messages 11B

- *What interpretive techniques and information are appropriate in this location?*
    - ✐ Collections Survey 11C

Completing this worksheet will help trainees shape the techniques and content of their casual interpretation efforts.

C. INITIATING MESSAGE-BASED CONVERSATIONS

Interaction is the element at the core of all good interpretation. Casual interpretation is especially well suited to creating conversations with visitors. There are several ways to initiate conversational interpretation.

- *How might you attract a visitor's attention without saying anything?*
    - ✐ Initiating Message-Based Conversations 11D

Props, actions, and good questions all can help to engage visitors in a dialogue. The first step is to identify how a good question is formulated. Then create questions that will initiate conversations for each collection.

   👁 Qualities of Good Questions 11E
   ✐ Identifying Questions 11F

- *How what we know about writing good questions help us initiate message-based questions?*

    ✎ Using Questions to Convey Messages 11G

- *How can we utilize visitor comments and questions to personalize and prolong the interaction?*

    ◯ The Chain of Interpretation 11H

- *What comments were (or could have been) difficult or controversial? How might you address a visitor misperception without being confrontational?*

Structured Interpretation: Chapter 12

Each step of this outline should be covered for every one of the programs that trainees are learning.

A. INCORPORATING CONVERSATION INTO EXISTING INTERPRETIVE PROGRAMS

    ◯ Incorporating Conversation Into Existing Interpretive Programs 12A

- *How are the elements of interpretation being successfully employed in this program?*

- *What are the challenges of this program?*

- *How can we use interpretive strategies (props, actions, questions) to overcome the challenges?*

B. THE ROLE OF TRANSITIONS

What is the role of transitions in structured interpretation?

    ◉ The Role of Transitions 12B

    ◉ Qualities of Transitions 12C

    ✎ Tour Transitions that Reinforce Theme and Messages 12D

Adding Value; Applying Interpretive Techniques to Content Presentations: Chapter 13

Whenever content presentations or resources are presented, here and throughout training, ask trainees to apply the lessons learned.

How can interesting, new factual ideas be shared with visitors through conversation and interaction?

    ◯ Applying Interpretive Techniques to Content Presentations 13A

Have trainees record their answers on worksheet

    ◯ Applying Interpretive Techniques to Content Presentations 13B

The Value of Evaluation: Chapter 14

What does successful interpretation look like at this museum?
How do we know we've succeeded as interpreters?

Evaluation offers feedback about whether we are reaching our goals. It also helps both interpreter and trainer improve the skills they need to connect visitors to the site.

Module 2 Training Outline:
Applying Interactive Techniques to Interpretive Opportunities

The Value of Evaluation 14A

Share and discuss selected evaluation interpreter evaluation tools, such as samples 3D, 3E, and 3F.

As trainers, we are committed to improving our skills and supporting you in a variety of ways. Please complete this training evaluation form to let us know how to enhance your training experience.

Distribute an evaluation form, such as sample 4A. Trainees who plan to complete Module 3 should wait and evaluate the entire training session.

CHAPTER 11 • Casual Interpretation:
Informal Conversations with Visitors

Casual interpretation occurs when an interpreter (staff or volunteer) has an impromptu exchange with a visitor. This interaction is not a scheduled program, does not require a prolonged time commitment, and may be initiated by either the interpreter or the visitor. But it does provide the interpreter with a unique opportunity to share new ideas or information about the museum's mission and messages. Casual interpretation can be an extremely powerful tool, but the interpreter must know how to engage the visitor, invite participation, and listen for opportunities to connect with the individual on a personal level.

In this chapter, trainees will learn how to initiate a conversation that can reveal the museum's messages about a collection. The informal nature of message-based conversation lends itself to a more personalized interaction and a positive visitor experience. Naturally, these conversations have the greatest impact when the interactions take place near the collections. Trainers should emphasize that although conversation can be an excellent educational tool, not every visitor will want to engage in a learning dialogue. But visitors do not have to converse to recall, process, and apply ideas to their lives; even those who are listening to conversational interpretation have great potential to learn. A visitor's body language—for example, refusing to make eye contact or physically distancing herself from the interpreter—can indicate that she does not wish to interact. Interpreters should be approachable but shouldn't force a conversation.

To help trainees understand this informal interpretive technique, highlight the differences between structured interpretation and casual interpretation (see overhead 11A). *Structured interpretation* is premeditated, controlled by set time limits, uses a presentation outline that includes layers of information, and designates where the interaction will occur. *Casual interpretation* is spontaneous, takes as long as the visitor's schedule allows, and has a loose thematic emphasis that capitalizes on concepts evident in nearby collections. Of course, museums also can determine the location for casual interpretation by assigning an interpreter to a given area where learning conversations are most likely to occur.

Both types of interpretation are more likely to succeed if they have themes and messages. Like interpretive programs, planning for casual interpretation should begin with ideas for initiating interactions based on a predetermined theme and messages. Overhead 11B defines themes and messages so trainees can understand their value, even when someone else has created them. Refer to the theme and messages trainers identified for each collection in chapter 2, using worksheet 1D, Identifying Themes and Messages.

Since interpreters often are assigned to a specific area or collection, trainees will find it helpful to visit such a location to gather ideas and impressions and focus their interpretation. During this activity, use the Collection/Exhibit Survey Worksheet (11C), which reinforces the Resource Survey in chapter 9.

Then ask the trainees to generate ideas for initiating message-based conversations. As highlighted in worksheet 11D, these might include asking provocative questions or using actions (e.g., striking the same pose as a subject in a painting) or props associated with the message.

Overhead 11E identifies the basic elements of a good question. A good question should be open-ended; if a visitor can answer a question with a simple "yes or no," the interaction will be stifled. A good question allows the visitor to respond without fear of being wrong. Using words that validate the visitor's perspective—whatever it may be—means there is less chance of creating a negative experience. For example, an interpreter might ask a question with qualifying words, such as, "What do you *think* the artist wants us to look at?" or "How *might* our understanding of Western history be different without these pioneer journals?" Finally, it encourages people to think about their personal experiences and internalize new ideas.

Worksheet 11F identifies the types of questions that encourage the visitor to create a "minds-on" experience by recalling, processing, and applying information. Worksheet 11G helps trainees write questions that can initiate message-based interaction or conversations. An interpreter who creates and uses effective questions will find great success in engaging visitors and, eventually, she should compile her own list of "good questions" and share it with colleagues.

Once a visitor's interest is sparked, it is important to keep her involved in the conversation. While continued use of questions, props, and actions is helpful, the interpreter also must be an extraordinary listener. The Chain of Interpretation (exercise 11H) is designed to help interpreters feel more comfortable about integrating visitor comments into their interpretive programs. In this exercise, trainees play the roles of interpreters and visitors. The "interpreter's" objective is to listen and look for ways to include the "visitor's" comments in the interpretive exchange; confirming the accuracy of the comments during this exercise is less important. This not only creates a personalized experience but, by validating her observations and perceptions, also keeps the visitor engaged in learning.

After completing the role-play exercise, discuss strategies for addressing "difficult visitor" comments while continuing the chain of interpretation. For example, it is important to address immediately a visitor comment such as "the Holocaust never happened." A way to do this politely is to say, "Thank you for your comment. However, museum staff (the interpreter could also specify scholars or experts) have done considerable research to find factual evidence to support (the facts you want to convey)." Even less serious statements such as "Elvis is still alive" should be addressed immediately. Ask the trainees if they have other examples or suggestions for addressing difficult visitor comments.

When appropriate, discuss recurring misperceptions or incorrect statements with staff or community experts on the given subject and develop an "official viewpoint of the museum." For example, at one museum, visitors often disagreed with the institution's position on natural restoration efforts. The interpretive staff worked with staff scientists to develop an official viewpoint that showed that the museum's methods were based on current scientific research. In this way, the interpreter no longer had to "defend" but could instead offer evidence for the museum's position.

Using these basic techniques, an interpreter can practice message-based casual interpretation in any museum location. Information desk attendants, concessionaires, and phone operators also can incorporate the techniques into their interactions with visitors. Becoming comfortable with casual interpretation may take time, but it is an invaluable tool for conveying messages to visitors, particularly those who don't plan to participate in more structured interpretive programs.

Characteristics of Structured & Casual Interpretation

Overhead 11A

Structured	versus	Casual
• Commitment and expectations **high** for participant		• Commitment and expectations **low** for participant
• Program begins at **scheduled time**		• Interaction begins with **opportunity**
• Time **commitment** necessary		• **Any time** available can be effective
• Has **beginning, middle, and end**		• Can pick up at **any point**
• More **formal** approach accepted		• **Informal** approach or interaction ideal
• More **complex**, layered, or sequential information conveyed		• **Quick** introductions, messages, and parting thoughts

Theme: the "big idea," what you want the visitor to take away. It answers the question, "so what?"

Messages: Learning ideas or objectives that illustrate the theme through supporting evidence. Messages focus ideas!

Collection/Exhibit Survey

Worksheet 11C

Note: Designed to be used with projects still in development, this worksheet also can be used with existing collections and exhibits.

Name of Collection/Exhibit:

Theme ("big idea") to be communicated:

What was your first impression of this collection/exhibit?

Where is the greatest visitor interest likely to be (and why)?

What stories are best told here, and where should they be told?

Who is likely to be connected to or most invested in this collection/exhibit?

What are the challenges of interpreting this collection/exhibit (observed and overheard)?

What might be the public perception of this collection/exhibit (expectations, misperceptions, etc.)?

Which museums/collections/exhibits are associated with this one, due to topic or location? Where are the connections?

What universal meanings are similar to or associated with this collection/exhibit?

List programs (or roles) for the interpreter:

Personal interpretation offers a unique opportunity to initiate casual conversations and interactions with visitors and still communicate important information. The following exercises will help you select props, determine actions, and formulate questions that can serve as the catalysts for these interactions.

A. Begin by determining **where** you want or anticipate the interaction to occur.

B. Write the **theme** ("big idea") and **messages** (important supporting ideas) of the location, exhibit, or collection where interaction will take place.

C. Brainstorm about **props** that can be used to illustrate that theme or message and attract attention.

D. Brainstorm about **actions** that can be used to initiate conversation about the theme or message.

E. To create effective **questions**, review overhead 11E and complete worksheets 11F and 11G.

LOCATION/EXHIBIT:

Theme:

Message 1:

Props: _____ Actions: _____
       _____   _____
       _____   _____

Message 2:

Props: _____ Actions: _____
       _____   _____
       _____   _____

Message 3:

Props: _____ Actions: _____
       _____   _____
       _____   _____

Good Questions:

- **cannot be answered "Yes" or "No"**
  Ask open-ended questions.

- **don't have a "right" or "wrong" answer**
  Use qualifying words, such as "think," "might," and "hypothetically."

- **relate to a visitor comment or provoke thought about the theme or messages**
  Make sure the question serves a purpose; don't get caught in an endless cycle of questions.

- **encourage visitors to recall, process, and/or apply ideas or previous experiences**
  Ask visitors about their personal experiences.

Remember: You don't have to have the answer(s) to a good question!

Identify each type of question in the following examples as:

> **R** . . . if it asks visitor to recall, identify, or enumerate
>
> **P** . . . if it asks visitor to process, analyze, or compare data
>
> **A** . . . if it asks visitor to apply, predict, or theorize

QUESTION TOOLBOXES

Recall	**Process**	**Application**
Counting	Analyze	Finding examples
Describing	Classify	Hypothesizing/Predicting
Identifying	Compare	Inventing
Listing	Contrast	Generalizing
Matching	Analogies (how is *x* like *y*)	Imagining
Observing	Organizing	Applying a principle

Type   Interpreter's Questions

_____1. What household objects can you see in the background of this photograph?

_____2. How do you think this landscape will look in 2020?

_____3. How many different recycled materials do you see in this sculpture?

_____4. What evidence do we have that people lived here over 200 years ago?

_____5. What do you think the people are doing in this painting?

_____6. How might this object have been used by a settler 100 years ago?

_____7. In what ways do crystals and diamonds differ?

_____8. When was the last time you saw a monarch butterfly in your neighborhood?

_____9. How do you think our lives would be different without museums?

_____10. If you could hear what was happening in this painting, what would it sound like?

_____11. How is a wetland like a sponge?

_____12. How might the pioneers that arrived here in 1890 dress differently than we do today?

Worksheet 11G

Visitors who recall facts, process data, and apply ideas are more likely to derive meaning from their experience than those who simply respond "yes" or "no" to the questions they are asked. Planning for successful interpretive interaction includes creating thoughtful questions. The following exercise will help to plan questions that will initiate message-based interaction or conversations.

A. **Record the theme and messages** for a desired location or collection in the designated boxes below to use as a reference during the activity.

B. **Create questions** that will initiate conversation related to that message.

C. **Indicate** how your question asks the visitor to *Recall* (R), *Process* (P), or *Apply* (A) ideas in the shaded box; it can be a combination of the three. (Reference the Question Toolboxes on page 111.)

Theme:

R/P/A

Message 1

1.

2.

3.

Message 2

1.

2.

3.

Message 3

1.

2.

3.

Need:

☐ collection of objects relevant to museum (or whimsical, if preferred) to be interpreted and discussed by groups

☐ entire group exercise; volunteers serve as interpreters or visitors

Goal: This interactive exercise is designed to help interpreters become more comfortable about integrating visitor comments into their interpretive programs. This creates a chain of information that unites the visitor's interests or knowledge with the museum's educational goals.

Here is how it works:

- Interpreters are divided into groups of three for a role-playing exercise: one person is the interpreter; the other two are visitors.
- The visitors are invited to look at the collection of objects that will be the focus of the activity; these objects can be random toys and represent an imaginary museum of the trainer's choice.
- One visitor makes a comment to another visitor regarding the collection (a personal memory, observation, or comparison).
- The other visitor responds to that comment.
- The interpreter integrates the comments of the visitors into the interpretation, and in so doing, involves them in the interpretation.

What the trainer needs to do:

- Identify that the volunteers are either visitors or interpreters at a _____ museum (this can be a fictitious institution).
- Explain the goal of the exercise—to practice integrating visitor comments in interpretation.
- Model the exercise for the trainees.
- Ask for questions to clarify the goals of the exercise. The facts about the objects are not as important as the process of hearing and incorporating visitor comments.
- Divide the group into smaller groups of three.
- Give groups different objects, activities, or assign to different areas in the exhibit/collection.
- Ask groups to identify roles, and provide cues so they can switch roles at intervals during the exercise.
- Monitor the groups to check for success and challenges that arise.
- Ask the successful group(s) to repeat their exercise(s) for the whole group.
- Respond to questions and summarize the exercise goals by using examples.

Adapted from an activity developed by the Visitor Research Team, Public Programs Division, Winterthur Museum, Garden, and Library, Winterthur, Del.

CHAPTER 12 • # Structured Interpretive Programs: Engaging Captive Audiences

This chapter refers to the museum's best interpretive programs, which trainers identified using the Program Inventory and Assessment Worksheet in chapter 2. This gives interpreters an opportunity to transform existing programs by incorporating the concepts of conversation, interaction, and inquiry discussed throughout Module 1 and in the casual interpretation section of Module 2. Trainers may find that the programs they have selected lack themes and messages. As such, themes and messages for each should be identified prior to the training exercises in this chapter. (See exercise 1C and worksheet 1D in chapter 1 for guidance.)

Integrating conversation elements into new or ongoing interpretive programs (see exercise 12A) can take time, but the efforts will make the visitor experience more positive. Trainers should introduce one program at a time, review its theme and messages with trainees, and then facilitate a discussion on how the program's location connects to the theme and messages. (Note: if the location does not relate to theme and messages, think about finding a more appropriate setting.) The next step is to review the A.R.T. of Interpretation—the audience, the resources, and the best techniques for delivery—as it relates to this program.

Share what is known about the potential audience and how these visitors might influence the content and techniques used in the delivery of the interpretation. Next provide opportunities for trainees to learn the facts (resources) that support the presentations; this can be done through expert lectures, videos, and resource materials provided during training. However, understanding the audience and knowing about the available resources are only the building blocks for an effective program. Trainees also must apply what they have learned through activities (techniques) that reinforce how to communicate those important facts. Ask experienced interpreters to model the programs, and give the group opportunities to discuss what worked well and what they might do differently. Trainees can review worksheet 11D to discuss message-based props and actions and worksheet 11G to determine questions for conversation, interaction, and inquiry.

The use of transitions is another helpful technique that can be a critical component of a structured interpretive experience. Transitions help interpreters connect ideas and keep the visitor involved when there is a lull in the presentation, a new concept is being introduced, or the tour group is moving from one location to another. Overhead 12B explores the role or function of transitions, and overhead 12C lists the qualities of effective transitions. Trainees can use worksheet 12D to devise transitions that might help focus thinking or connect ideas as a group moves around during an interpretive tour.

After the techniques have been discussed, the exercise can conclude with role-playing activities in which trainees integrate some of the new techniques or ideas into aspects of the program.

> **Need:**
>
> ☐ Volunteers (preferably veteran interpreters) to deliver existing interpretive programs

Goal: This exercise is designed to revisit existing interpretive programs and discover ways to infuse interaction or conversation into the delivery.

What the trainer needs to do:

1. Write a description (program write-up) of the selected program for distribution to trainees. (See Elements of Effective Program Write-ups in chapter 17.)

2. Review the program's theme and messages as a group.

3. Discuss the program's location(s) and make object/visual/concept connections between the location and the theme and messages.

4. Go over the background of the program using the A.R.T. of Interpretation.

   A: Review the **A**udience for the program and discuss special needs or issues.

   R: Provide opportunities to learn the content through various **R**esources

   (e.g., guest lecture, video(s), handouts, books, and research).

   T: Review **T**echniques for delivering the program:

   • Have veteran interpreter deliver the entire or pieces of the program.

   • Discuss as a group whether theme and messages emerged clearly.

   • Discuss aspects that worked well.

   • Discuss what changes would make the program more engaging.

   • Revisit ✐ worksheet 11A and brainstorm about additional props or actions to initiate interaction or serve as a bridge between ideas.

   • Revisit ✐ worksheet 11C and ask the group to write questions that can introduce the messages.

   • Introduce the concept of transitions; review and discuss overhead 12B and 12C.

   • Discuss the use of transitions in the modeled program; solicit suggestions or examples that worked.

   • If the program is a tour, ask trainees to use worksheet 12D to record some of their ideas for transitions.

   • Ask for volunteers to role-play, applying new techniques used during the exercise.

(continues on next page)

Exercise 12A

5. Review the program write-up as a group and encourage trainees to note which new ideas worked well.

6. Repeat this process for every interpretive program for which the trainees will be responsible.

7. Revise program write-ups to reflect changes and best suggestions for incorporating conversation, interaction, and inquiry.

We use transitions to:

- **generate anticipation** for what will be seen or heard next

- **invite visitor involvement** (mental and sensory)

- **create a bridge** or connection between ideas

- **provide directive** or focus during group movement

- **allow visitors to apply their own experiences** and knowledge

- **create a foundation** for new information

Overhead 12C

A transition:

- **relates to theme (the "big idea"), not the specifics of the object**

    e.g.: Both of these plants rely on insect pollinators to reproduce. How might the observable differences between the flowers' structure and colors show that they are pollinated by different insects?

- **hints at reason for the next stop** on the tour

    e.g.: If you think this is an unusual example of expressionism, let's see how it compares to this painting by a different artist.

- **includes visitor comments**

    e.g.: People may celebrate this holiday like Dan's family or in one of many other ways. Let's see how people from other countries celebrate.

- **can be action or activity**

    e.g.: As we move to the next stop, count how many of the objects we pass are made of the same materials we observed here.

- **is only one or two sentences**

- **uses questions, guided interaction/directives, provocative statements, summaries, and analogies**

Theme (and Messages):

Stop Location:_____

Theme connection:

Transition:

Stop Location:_____

Theme Connection:

Transition:

Stop Location:_____

Theme Connection:

Transition:

Stop Location:_____

Theme Connection:

CHAPTER 13 • Adding Value: Applying Interpretive Techniques to Content Presentations

During training programs, content experts often are invited to make presentations that emphasize how important it is for interpreters to have relevant and accurate facts that they can share with visitors. In fact, these types of "behind-the-scenes/meet the expert" presentations are a primary reason volunteer interpreters choose to get involved with an institution. The trainer should not only provide these experiences, but also should show trainees how to apply the interpretive techniques learned in Module 1 to the content-related presentations (in addition to facts learned from videos, articles, etc.).

For example, curators often are invited to share their knowledge through lectures or gallery tours as a part of interpreter training. These personal experiences provide excellent anecdotes that trainees can share with visitors. But the trainer needs to schedule time at the end of the presentation to work with trainees to process those experiences. It's more important to determine strategies for connecting facts to the visitors' lives than to regurgitate memorized anecdotes.

If the new content information is offered to trainees as part of a live training presentation, designate 20 minutes at the end for a discussion with the group using exercise 13A. If the new information will be obtained outside of training, where a group discussion cannot be facilitated, encourage trainees to complete worksheet 13B. Long after the training is completed, this worksheet can remind interpreters how to process new facts and make them relevant to visitors.

Applying Interpretive Techniques to Content Presentations

Exercise 13A

Need:

☐ 1 flip chart, markers

☐ flip chart or overhead stating the relevant themes and messages of the collection, exhibit, or program (e.g., history gallery theme and messages during presentation by history curator)

Goal: To illustrate the importance of utilizing conversational interpretive techniques to make collections content relevant and meaningful to museum visitors.

What the trainer needs to do:

What were some of the exciting, new, compelling ideas or facts that the expert/resource offered? Why did these ideas interest you?
Solicit answers from the group and record on the flip chart.

Which ideas might enhance the visitor's understanding or appreciation for the collection, program, etc.?
On the flip chart, circle the ideas that would be appropriate for sharing with visitors. Then discuss connections to the theme and messages.

　　　👁 Theme and Messages (related to collection/program)

How do the new ideas/information relate to or illustrate the theme and messages of this collection, program, etc.?
Review each idea and determine which message it helps to reinforce.

How can these ideas become meaningful to visitors? How can we make connections to their lives? What are the universal qualities of each idea?
Brainstorm about the universal qualities of each idea and ways to make connections to the visitors' lives.

What questions might engage visitors in a message-based conversation about these ideas?
Ask the group to devise questions, share them with the group, and then discuss ways to improve them.

　　　👁 Qualities of Good Questions (overhead 11C)

Are there new or existing props that might help visitors connect with these ideas?
Ask the group to suggest useful props and talk about possible ways of obtaining desired new props.

Thank the trainees for their participation and remind them that this activity was designed to help them effectively share their interest in this content in a way that is meaningful to visitors.

Name of the Expert/Resource (video, article, etc.):

Date/Time:

This presentation relates to the following:

Collection/Exhibit:_____

Program:_____

---

1. What were some of the exciting, new, compelling ideas that the expert/resource offered? Why did these ideas interest you?

2. Which ideas might enhance the visitor's understanding or appreciation for the collection, exhibit, program, etc.?

3. How does each idea relate to the theme and messages of this collection, exhibit, program, etc.?

4. How can these ideas become meaningful to visitors? How can we make connections to visitors' lives? What are some universal qualities of these ideas?

5. What ideas might give clarification to someone new to this subject?

6. What questions could we ask visitors to engage them in a message-based conversation about these ideas?

7. Are there new or existing props that could help visitors connect with these ideas?

Interpretation is a voyage of discovery in the field of human emotions and intellectual growth, and it is hard to foresee that time when the interpreter can confidently say, "Now we are wholly adequate to our task."

Freeman Tilden • Interpreting Our Heritage (1957)

CHAPTER 14 • # The Power of Evaluation: Improving Our Interpretation

The final chapter in Module 2 introduces trainees to the interpreter evaluation tools selected by the trainer in chapter 3. This lesson demonstrates how evaluation improves both the skills of the interpreters and those who train and support them—by providing guidance on modifying and/or improving future training. The evaluation tools should both reinforce the expectations established in the interpreters' job descriptions and the lessons learned from the training thus far.

No matter which evaluation tool(s) you choose, explain the reasons for your selection to the trainees, comparing and contrasting the two forms discussed here. Self-evaluation allows an interpreter to assess her own performance and reflect on her successes, weaknesses, and areas for growth. See chapter 3 for sample evaluation forms focusing on both general and specific, tour-related skills. External evaluation incorporates supervisor, mentor, and/or peer reviews and observations. Another person can provide valuable insight on how an interpreter might improve her interaction with visitors. Sample 3E (see chapter 3) can be used by peer reviewers. Sample 3F might be used by a supervisor or mentor as she observes an interpreter. Ideally a trainer will select and use more than one tool to diversify the feedback given to the trainee.

Evaluation often is perceived as a quality-control exercise that ensures that interpreters are delivering "satisfactory" interpretation. While quality control is important, supervisors also should use evaluation to determine how their own leadership, training, or support of interpreters can be improved. When interpreters feel supported and valued in their work, staff and volunteer retention is likely to increase. Using the Value of Evaluation (overhead 14A), review the mutual benefits of evaluation with trainees.

An evaluation of the training program itself demonstrates the museum's commitment to creating the most effective learning experience for its interpreters; see sample evaluation form 4A in chapter 4. Review comments offered by participants to see how the training might better prepare interpreters to engage visitors in learning dialogues.

Overhead 14A

Evaluation:

- **encourages ongoing growth** and desire to gain new skills/knowledge

- **identifies areas of weakness** and potential support

- **offers feedback** to trainers about how to modify or improve training

- **provides insight** about how trainers can improve their communication and teaching skills

- **encourages ongoing interaction** between interpreters and trainers/supervisors/mentors

- **reinforces** the concept that every interpreter-supervisor relationship has **room for improvement**

- **ensures overall quality control** and accountability for the development and delivery of, and training for, an interpretive program

Key:

Questions for trainees

👁 Overhead

( ) Interactive Exercise

✍ Worksheet

Training Tools Used in Module 3 (in the order in which they appear).

( ) Avoiding Programming Pitfalls 15A

👁 Why Do Interpretive Programs Fail? 15 B, 15C, 15D

✍ Program Strengths and Challenges 15E

👁 What Motivates Program Development 15F

✍ Interpretive Program Worksheet 16A

👁 Defining Theme and Messages 11B

( ) Theme and Message Development 1C

✍ Identifying Themes and Messages 1D

( ) Tangible, Intangible, and Universal Connections 7C

👁 Qualities of Good Questions 11E

✍ Identifying Questions 11F

✍ Using Questions to Convey Messages 11G

👁 Elements of Effective Program Write-Ups 17A

✍ Interpretive Program Write-up Template 17B

Training Introduction: Chapter 5 (review)

- Explain to trainees how the training day will be structured and how their basic needs will be met in terms of bathroom breaks, food, rest breaks, etc. (*Note:* Depending on the museum's schedule, the training "day" may take place in a single afternoon or in a two-day session. Trainers can shorten the schedule, if necessary, by asking trainees to complete some assignments as homework.)

- Reinforce the idea of conversation as the premise behind interpretive training.

- Review *goals* of Module 3:

  - Provide brainstorming tools to guide interpretive program development.

  - Highlight the value of applying interactive techniques learned in Training Modules 1 and 2.

  - Review the components of an effective program write-up to ensure effective dissemination of theme and messages.

- Add other applicable goals developed by trainer in chapter 4

Module 3
Training Outline: Developing New Interpretive Programs

Avoiding Programming Pitfalls: Chapter 15

A. WHY DO INTERPRETIVE PROGRAMS FAIL?

- *Think of a program—either one you have delivered or one you've seen—that you consider "successful." What were the reasons or qualities that made it successful?*
(Record all answers on flip chart.)

Keep these qualities in mind. As we try to create successful programs, it is also helpful to talk about why programs fail.

- *Recalling the work on evaluation we completed in Module 2, let's revisit the question: How do you know when a program has succeeded?*
    - ( ) Avoiding Programming Pitfalls 15A
    - 👁 Why Do Interpretive Programs Fail? 15B, 15C, 15D
    - 📝 Program Strengths and Challenges 15E

B. WHAT MOTIVATES PROGRAM DEVELOPMENT?

- *Think of a recently developed or delivered program. What was the motivation that influenced the selection of the content and techniques?*
    - 👁 *What Motivates Program Development 15F*

We create programs for many different reasons. But whatever the reason, it is important to acknowledge the motivations behind a program and to make the necessary adjustments to ensure success. Slight alterations to the program's content focus or techniques used can vastly improve the opportunities for connecting with visitors.

The Interpretive Program Worksheet: Chapter 16

A. INTRODUCTION TO THE INTERPRETIVE PROGRAM WORKSHEET

This worksheet helps interpreters develop program themes and messages and provides a framework for creating both structured and casual interpretation. It will allow us to brainstorm ideas for a new program while providing focus for the program's content development. This worksheet reflects the fusion of the theory and techniques presented in Modules 1 and 2.

📝 Interpretive Program Worksheet 16A

The worksheet is divided into three sections:

1. *Program Background:* collection/event concept, target audience, program topic, learning objective, emotional objective, behavioral objective, tangible and intangible concepts, universal meanings, public perception considerations, learning location and program time(s)
2. *Program Focus:* theme and messages
3. *Content Considerations:* interactive/illustrative tools, key questions, program title, introduction, conclusion, parting thoughts

B. Program Background Information

Ask trainees to review the definitions on part 2 of worksheet 16A. Then ask them to answer the following questions on part 1 of the worksheet.

• *What is the topic of the related exhibit or event?*

Answering this question will provide the **context** for the environment in which the program will take place.

• *Who is the program for?*

The **target audience** should be based on the context for the program and the known or expected visitation.

• *In general, what is this program about?*

The big-picture **concepts** should be stated early in the program development process.

• *What do we want visitors to know?*

Determine what information is most important for the visitors to **learn** from the program.

• *What do I want the visitor to feel?*

Determine whether there are **emotions** that the trainees would like visitors to associate with the program.

• *What do I want the visitor to do?*

Consider ways to invite the visitor to take part in a hands-on activity or to take action (during or after the visit) that reinforces the purpose of the program.

• *How can we help visitors connect with the real and meaningful aspects of the collections?*
    () Tangible, Intangible, and Universal Connections 7C

Ask trainees to consider the tangible, intangible, and universal qualities of the content so they can help visitors relate to the messages.

• *What might be the public perception of your program's content? Is the content controversial? Are there opposing points of view? What are the commonly held myths about the subject?*

Brainstorming with another trainee about potential perceptions or misperceptions can be useful for anticipating and developing appropriate responses to visitors' potential concerns, beliefs, or reactions.

• *Where will the program take place within the exhibit/museum?*

Ask trainees to identify the **location** that best suits the program's purpose. Sometimes there is no choice because a certain location (e.g., a demonstration area) must be used for a program.

• *When will the program occur?*

The **proposed time** for the program is an important consideration and should be based on when the target audience is most likely to be visiting the museum.

C. PROGRAM FOCUS

• *Why do you think the next step is to determine the program's theme and messages?*

The theme and messages provide focus for gathering additional information. The messages may change slightly as new information is gathered, but the central ideas should still drive development efforts, rather than be created after the research/brainstorming is complete.

👁 Defining Theme and Messages 11B

• *What is the difference between a program concept and a theme?*

() Theme and Message Development 1C

✎ Identifying Themes and Messages 1D

D. CONTENT CONSIDERATIONS

• *What props or interactive tools will help visitors learn about the program's messages?*

List props or other illustrative tools that will help reinforce each message.

• *What questions might engage visitors in message-based conversations?*

👁 Qualities of Good Questions 11E

✎ Identifying Questions 11F

✎ Using Questions to Convey Messages 11G

• *What title might grab visitors' attention by addressing a common misperception, appealing to their known interests, presenting a challenge, or promising new information or experiences?*

The title can draw on information revealed during the brainstorming section of the Program Background worksheet; it should refer to the program theme.

Ask trainees share their title ideas with the group. Discuss which ones might be most appealing to visitors and possible ways to enhance their potential.

• *Will you use your introduction to hook the visitor? What will keep visitors interested in your theme?*

The introduction should capture visitors' interest and tell them what to expect by introducing the theme of the program.

> • *How will the conclusion refer to the program's messages? How can you get visitors to recall, process, and apply important ideas from the program?*

The conclusion should reiterate the theme and remind visitors about the program's main messages—that's the information you want visitors to take away with them.

> • *How will you encourage ongoing dialogue among visitors as they leave the program and the museum?*

Parting thoughts are intended to continue the dialogue about the messages of the program.

Disseminating Programming Information: Chapter 17

A. ELEMENTS OF AN EFFECTIVE PROGRAM WRITE-UP

> • *Why are program write-ups important?*

(Solicit answers and record on flip chart.)

> • *If you only had 60 minutes to prepare for an interpretive program, what type of information would you want or need?*

(Write responses on flip chart.)

Other interpreters have been asked what they would need; this form is a compilation of their answers:

> 👁 Elements of Effective Program Write-Ups 17A

B. DEVELOPING AN INSTITUTIONAL PROGRAM WRITE-UP TEMPLATE

> • *If there is a current program write-up format and/or support information, does it give an interpreter the information she needs?*

(Compare to list of needs and wants.)

> • *Based on what interpreters need (and the format currently used), can we structure a program write-up to more effectively prepare interpreters to engage visitors in dialogue?*
> 📝 Interpretive Program Write-up Template 17B

CHAPTER 15 • # Avoiding Programming Pitfalls

A critical part of learning about program development is determining which factors contribute to, and which stand in the way of, successful interpretation. Exercise 15A gives trainees an opportunity to share their experiences with both program success and failure. Begin by asking trainees how they can measure the success of a program. Some common responses might include positive feedback, high attendance, visitor smiles and/or participation, knowledge retention (measured by verbal or written survey), or word-of-mouth recommendations, such as "I came to this program because my neighbors enjoyed it when they visited." While not all measures accurately reflect success (e.g., smiles can be misleading), these different methods—including surveys, attendance, or income—do provide valuable indications of whether or not a program is working.

Then ask trainees to talk about programs that have failed; this helps them learn about common and avoidable programming pitfalls. Generally, programs fail in three categories: inappropriate content, lack of preparation, or issues related to implementation. As museum practitioners know, it isn't just visitors who suffer when programs don't work; staff morale and the museum's image also can be affected. Overheads 15B-D elaborate on some of the reasons programs fail.

Worksheet 15E asks trainees to assess the motivation behind a current or future program, and determine ways to capitalize on that motivation's strengths or develop strategies to overcome the program's challenges. This worksheet also will help them complete the Interpretive Program Worksheet in chapter 16.

A program's success or failure often can be traced back to its original motivation (see overhead 15B). Some motivations almost guarantee success; for example, visitors regularly ask questions about the box turtle and want to get a closer look. Others inherently present a challenge; for example, the board president has just returned from Disneyland and would like a costumed character to stroll through his favorite gallery. Remind trainees that although we cannot always control the reasons programs are created, we can anticipate the pitfalls and minimize the challenges.

Trainers should encourage trainees to take notes on worksheet 15E as you discuss the contents of overhead 15F, a list of motivations that might inspire new programs. This list is based on responses gathered from educators during research for this manual and is organized according to likelihood of success. For example, a program created in response to visitor interest in painting A is more likely to succeed than one that was created about painting B, a personal favorite of a particular staff person. As mentioned earlier, all motivations have the potential to inspire a successful program, as long as the program developer also finds ways to make connections between the audience and the collection/exhibit.

Need:

☐ 1 volunteer to record responses on a flip chart

☐ 2 flip charts or writing surfaces and markers, chalk, etc.

Goal: Trainees will assess the reasons why programs succeed and fail, the value of various motivations behind program creation, and how to enhance the potential for success.

What the trainer needs to do:
Ask trainees to talk about how they know when a program has succeeded.
Solicit answers from the group and record on flip chart 1.

Ask the group to discuss why some programs fail. What factors inhibit success?
Solicit answers from the group and record on flip chart 2
　　　　👁 Why Do Interpretive Programs Fail? Overheads 15B, 15C, 15D

One of the main reasons a programs fails is because the motivation for developing it was inappropriate or incomplete. This next exercise builds on what we know about program failure and looks for the strengths that we can draw from the motivation behind every program.

Distribute ✐ worksheet 15E to trainees prior to discussion of overhead 15F.

Ask the group to think of a recently developed or delivered program. What was the motivation that influenced the selection of the content and techniques?
　　　　👁 What Motivates Program Development? Overhead 15F

Discuss each motivation and have trainees indicate which motivation(s) influenced their program. Ask trainees to record their ideas on the worksheet 15E.

Discuss the strengths and weaknesses of each source of motivation. While some motivations offer greater potential for success than others, every program can succeed.
Ask trainees to record their ideas on the worksheet.

Now that the group knows more about why programs fail, how will they change their programming plans?
Ask trainees to record their ideas on the worksheet.

Overhead 15B

Content Challenges

▸**Inappropriate** *motivation*: does not reflect audience needs for content information, the collection's value, or the museum's mission and messages

▸**Inappropriate** *audience*: does not take visitors' needs and skill levels into consideration

▸**Inappropriate** *content focus*: does not relate to collections

▸**Inappropriate** *technique*: delivery does not connect with audience or reflect interpreter's skills

▸**Inappropriate** *length*: amount of time not realistic based on audience needs

Overhead 15C

Preparation Challenges

- **Lack of *development time*:** staff did not or was not allowed to schedule enough time for planning
- **Lack of *training*:** interpreters were not given guidance on how to effectively deliver program
- **Lack of *accessible support materials*:** materials were not incorporated into program write-up
- **Lack of *administrative support*:** management did not give staff sufficient time or resources to complete their work
- **Lack of *funding*:** budget won't provide long-term support for the program
- **Lack of *publicity*:** failure to get the word to visitors, both at museum and off-site
- **Lack of *partnerships*:** staff, knowledge, or materials needed from outside source

Overhead 15D

Implementation Challenges

- ▸**Poor** *scheduling:* time for program does not coincide with peak visitation period

- ▸**Poor** *weather:* climate conditions deter visitation or make program difficult to deliver

- ▸**Poor** *location:* space does not reflect audience size, is hard to get to, lacks shelter, does not reflect program topic, does not provide access to supporting technology, etc.

- ▸**Inappropriate** *cost:* too much is prohibitive; too little doesn't cover program costs or creates the perception that the program is of little value

- ▸**Lack of staff** *enthusiasm* due to the existence of one or all of the above problems

> **Why do some programs fail? What factors inhibit success?**

Program Name/Topic:_____

1. Which motivation(s) influenced the development of this program? (See overhead 15F for explanations of each category.)

    ☐ Audience Expectation/Interest   ☐ Observed Need

    ☐ Collections Content   ☐ Unrelated Inspiration

    ☐ Technique Preference   ☐ Mystery Mandate

    ☐ Mission Related   ☐ Other_____

2. What strengths and challenges are inherent in the motivation(s)?

Strengths:

Challenges:

3. Based on what you now know about why programs fail, how will you change this program?

Content:

Preparation:

Implementation:

Overhead 15F

↦ **Audience Expectation/Interest**

Visitor requests, promised in printed materials, regular questions on subject

↦ **Collections Content (resources)**

Temporary exhibit, timely event/connection (e.g., birth of animal historical anniversary, restoration of object)

↦ **Technique Preference**

Desired/requested format for interpreting dictated content (storytelling, crafts, tour, etc.)

↦ **Mission Related**

Fulfills or communicates some aspect of the mission

↦ **Observed Need**

To fill a gap in information or redirect visitor interactions with collections

↦ **Unrelated Inspiration**

Preference/passion of person dictating or developing programs

↦ **Mystery Mandate**

Unexplained or unclear administrative/donor request

↦ **Other?**

[P]rograms and conversations derive their strength, flexibility, and connectedness from being human exercises. . . . Good museum programmers and engaged visitors surf on this social need, using it to bridge objects to people.

Michael Spock • Presence of Mind: Museums and the Spirit of Learning (1999)

CHAPTER 16 • The Interpretive Program Worksheet

This chapter focuses on the comprehensive task of creating an interpretive program, using the ideas and techniques explored in Modules 1 and 2. The Interpretive Program Worksheet (16A) helps trainees develop program themes and messages; tangible, intangible, and universal concepts; and learning, emotional, and behavioral objectives. It also provides a framework for creating both structured and casual interpretation and developing ideas and content for a new program. While the worksheet helps trainees think comprehensively about program elements, it cannot replace a complete program write-up, which will be addressed in chapter 17.

The worksheet is divided into three sections—Program Background, Program Focus, and Content Considerations. The trainer should present each section, one at a time, to the group of trainees. As each new section is introduced, review the relevant definitions listed in Defining the Interpretive Program, part 2 of worksheet 16A (pages 151-153).

PROGRAM BACKGROUND

This includes collection/exhibit context; target audience; program topic; learning, emotional, and behavioral objectives; tangible and intangible concepts; universal meanings; public perception considerations; learning location; and proposed time(s).

Begin by asking trainees to use the age-old questions "Who, What, Where, When, and How?" to determine the program's foundation. (The "Why" of the program will be answered in the worksheet's next section when the theme and messages are developed.) The first question should be, "What is the context or venue for the program?" As a program developer, the trainee should know if the program will be a part of a special event or an ongoing activity connected to a collection or exhibit. The context usually is evident from the program's title; for example, "Modern Art: 1950 to the Present," "Fall Harvest Festival," "Africa Explored; A Quest to Uncover History."

When the program context has been identified, trainees then should determine the target audience by answering the question, "Whom is this program for?" The audience should significantly shape the content. Unlike programs offered for known, predetermined audiences (e.g., a Spanish-speaking student group), those directed at casual visitors must have strategies for connecting with audiences diverse in age, ethnicity, and learning styles. Non-English speaking visitors, inter-generational groups, and visitors with disabilities all should be factored into the strategies selected for program delivery.

The concept provides a general idea of what the program content is about; it encompasses big ideas that must become more specific to result in a theme. For example, if the program topic is "Oregon History," a theme could be created by answering the question, "What do you want to tell visitors about Oregon history?"

The next step is to develop learning, emotional, and behavioral objectives, each of which addresses a different type of visitor experience. These objectives are based on research conducted in the 1950s by a committee of educational psychologists led by Benjamin Bloom. This team identified three domains of educational activity—cognitive (learning/knowing), affective (emotional/feeling), and psychomotor (behavioral/doing)— now referred to as Bloom's Taxonomy (Bloom, et al., 1964). Learning activities have greater potential to reach visitors when they blend and balance these domains to:
- provide information on the collection—the cognitive domain (knowing)
- evoke feelings about the collections or concepts that support the museum—the affective domain (feeling)
- facilitate sensory/participatory experiences that help people interact with the collection/exhibit—the psychomotor domain (doing)

The next set of background information shapes a program to be more personal and engaging by exploring the meanings and perceptions associated with its content. Tangible, intangible, and universal meanings help visitors create factual and emotional connections to the collection/exhibit. If trainees need a refresher or did not participate in Module 1, exercise 7C will show them how to address the tangible (concrete) concepts, intangible (abstract) concepts, and universal meanings that can make program content more relevant to every visitor.

Public perception also can influence a program's success. Ask trainees to brainstorm, perhaps in small groups, about how visitors might react to the proposed program topics. Thinking about whether the content might be associated with fear, childhood memories, media stories, or even religious beliefs can help trainees to anticipate reactions and be sensitive to visitors' feelings, while finding ways to introduce a new understanding.

The final steps in this section of the worksheet ask trainees to consider carefully where and when the program will be most successful. Identifying the program's location can increase effectiveness by capitalizing on strengths of the nearby collections and avoiding common programming pitfalls (e.g., overcrowding, noise). When selecting program times, take note of when the target audience is expected to visit the museum.

PROGRAM FOCUS

Once the program background has been determined, trainees can use what they've learned about the collection/exhibit and turn their attention to the program's focus—i.e., its theme and messages. As discussed in chapter 1, ideally the theme and messages will be developed in collaboration with curators, educators, and other staff experts. However, a new interpretive program may require a more specialized structure, one that both builds on the collection/exhibit theme and accomplishes the objectives of the interpretive program. This section of the worksheet asks the question, "Why should a visitor care about this program?" To help the trainees craft their responses, the trainer should review the definitions of theme and messages. The trainer also can refer to chapter 1, which includes exercises, worksheets, and sample forms to help trainees develop a theme and message structure for existing programs.

CONTENT CONSIDERATIONS

These include interactive/illustrative tools, key questions, program title, introduction, conclusion, and parting thoughts.

The rest of the Interpretive Program Worksheet focuses on techniques for illustrating the program messages. Ask trainees to brainstorm about ways to use props or exercises to reinforce the museum's messages, encourage visitors to use their senses, and give them opportunities to interact with objects that connect the messages to their lives.

Questions that invite visitors to recall, process, and apply the messages to their lives help to personalize the program and ultimately aid the learning process. If necessary, review overhead 11E and discuss the qualities of good questions. Worksheets 11F and 11G can help trainees write message-based questions that will encourage visitors to think about the program content. Asking trainees to develop a few key questions that could initiate a conversation will help them create a program write-up in chapter 17.

To capture the uniqueness and excitement of the program, the title should be determined only after trainees have completed the previous exercises. It should entice visitors, without being so vague or mysterious that it is intimidating. It should build expectations and suggest the benefits of attending the program. Give trainees an opportunity to draft titles and then discuss them as a group. When a title is suggested, others in the group should take on the role of the visitor and provide reactions. Some suggestions for helping trainees to refine titles include:
- make stronger connections to the collection
- suggesting the fun or knowledge that can be gained from the program
- use exciting language
- use words or analogies that are familiar to the visitor

The trainees' final task is to draft an introduction, conclusion, and parting thoughts for the program. The introduction must hook audience members and encourage them to participate, and also is when the theme should be communicated. To build expectations for the program, the messages can be referred to here, but the full explanation of the messages should unfold as a part of a compelling program.

The program conclusion should summarize the messages and refer back to the theme, the "big idea" you want visitors to take away with them. This may be an opportunity to ask questions that encourage visitors to recall messages or share what they've learned. Closing the program with some parting thoughts—simple statements, questions, or hand-outs (sheets, stickers, rewards)—encourages visitors to continue thinking about the theme even after they have left the museum.

Collection/Event Context:

Target Audience:

Program Topics:

Learning Objective:

Emotional Objective:

Behavioral Objective:

Tangible (concrete/intellectual) concepts: **Intangible** (abstract/emotional) concepts:

_____   _____

_____   _____

_____   _____

Universal meanings related to program:

Public perceptions of topic or content:

Learning Location:_____   Proposed Time(s):_____

Program Theme:

Messages:

1.

2.

3.

(continues on next page)

Interpretive Program Worksheet

Worksheet 16 A: Part 1

Interactive/Illustrative Tools:

Message 1   Message 2   Message 3

_____   _____   _____

_____   _____   _____

_____   _____   _____

Key Questions to introduce topic or engage audience in messages:

1.

2.

3.

4.

Program Title:

Introduction:

Conclusion:

Parting Thoughts:

This list of definitions will help you complete the Interpretive Program Worksheet, which is designed to provide guidance during interpretive program development. The definitions are listed in the order in which they appear on the worksheet and are organized based on whether they relate to Program Background, Program Focus, or Content Considerations. Although the worksheet can help develop theme-based interactive programming, it cannot replace, and should be completed before, the program write-up.

Program Background

Collection/Event Context: "What is the larger setting for the program? What is the collection or event about?"

The context typically is determined before the interpretive programs are developed and is usually evident from the program's title (e.g., "Modern Art: 1950 to the Present," "Fall Harvest Festival," "Africa Explored: A Quest to Uncover History"). The context establishes priorities and parameters that reinforce the goals of the site or event. It refers to the expectations created for visitors through text and/or tone of the title and promotional materials.

Target Audience: "Whom is this program for?"

The target audience is either the people who are already coming to your museum (e.g., families, school groups) or the people you would like to attract through a special program (e.g., Girl Scouts, senior tour groups).

Program Topics: "What is this program about?"

Program topics are the subject matter that shapes the theme. Topics (e.g.; Oregon history, basket weaving, forensic science, pollination) answer the question, "What information should be conveyed to visitors?" Topics are fragments, not complete thoughts or sentences. (Ham, 1992)

Learning Objective: "What do I want visitors to know?"

This objective is focused on having visitors be able to recall, list, or describe facts or items after a program is completed. Determining which facts you want visitors to retain is valuable, but we are more likely to make connections if we also identify how we want visitors to feel and act after the program. (Veverka, 1994)

Emotional Objective: "What do I want visitors to feel?"

Accounting for emotions is an important part of the decision-making process. If we are want to influence attitudes or behavior, we must strive to reach visitors emotionally. By considering how we want visitors to feel, we are more likely to create experiences that will influence their actions and the knowledge they gain.

Defining the Interpretive Program Worksheet

Worksheet 16A: Part 2

Behavioral Objective: "What do I want visitors to do?"
If we can inspire a visitor to take action, we have truly succeeded. When we encourage visitors to interact with the collections or become involved in the mission, we are making personal connections. Public involvement translates into long-term success. (Veverka, 1994)

Learning Location: "Where will this program be experienced?"
Identifying where the program will take place can increase effectiveness by allowing interpreters to capitalize on the area's strengths and avoid its pitfalls (e.g., overcrowding, noise).

Proposed Time(s): "When will the program occur?"
The time of the program can influence its content and nature. The ideal time for a program is based on the visitation patterns of the target audience. For example, if the desired audience is school groups, the program should be offered between 10 a.m. and 2 p.m. The proposed time(s) can specify start times for a structured tour, such as 3 p.m., or indicate a range of time when casual interpretation might occur, such as "between 1 and 3 p.m."

Tangible Concepts: How does something look, smell, feel (texture), etc.? What is (or can be) known by everyone about the concept/object through observation? These concepts help visitors make intellectual connections.

Intangible Concepts: How does something make an individual feel? What emotions or experiences does it relate to? Are there experiences someone might associate with the concept/object that could be included in the program? These abstract concepts are important for making emotional connections.

Universal Meanings: Concepts or ideas connected to the interpretive program that relate to everyday life and often reference family, change, history, work, reward, money, etc. Referring to these meanings in your dialogue can help make program content relevant to everyone in the audience.

Public Perception Considerations: Be aware of what the public may be thinking; everyone brings emotional baggage. Read the papers and understand current events that may influence visitor opinions, fears, and feelings.

Program Focus:

Program Theme: The theme is the "big idea" or overriding concept you want visitors to take away with them; it is a general statement that encompasses all the elements of the program. You can formulate the theme by completing this sentence: "If there is one thing I want the visitor to remember about this site/topic, it is that. . . . "

Messages: Messages offer supporting "evidence"—stories, experiences, concepts—that help to illustrate the theme. Limiting the number of messages to three increases the impact and retention of more specific ideas and helps to avoid confusion. The desired facts, emotions, or behaviors determined in the objectives above should be integrated into the messages. Specifically: "If I want visitors to understand the theme, it is important for them to know/feel/do. . . . "

Content Considerations:

Interactive/Illustrative Tools: These tools should be tangible opportunities (props) that invite visitors to use their senses to directly experience the message. Using props provides a focal point that visitors can associate with the message, and thus increases the potential for a meaningful and relevant experience.

Key Questions: Questions used throughout the program to engage visitors by asking them to process, compare, or internalize information. Not all of the questions need to be answered!

Program Title: The title for the program should be considered only after previous exercises have been completed. It should capture the program's uniqueness and excitement, build visitor expectations, and suggest the reward of attending.

Introduction: The beginning of a program must hook the audience into participating and communicate the theme. Interpreters can allude to the message by building expectations, but the full description of the message should unfold as a part of a compelling program.

Conclusion: The program conclusion should summarize your messages and refer back to the theme. This may be an opportunity to reinforce the messages by asking visitors to share what they have learned.

Parting Thoughts: This aspect of the program reinforces the "take-away" element of all programs. It can be simple statements, questions, or hand-outs (sheets, stickers, rewards) that encourage visitors to continue thinking about the message.

References

Bloom, Benjamin S.; Mesia, Bertram B.; and Krathwohl, David R.(1964). *Taxonomy of Educational Objectives* (two vols: *The Affective Domain* and *The Cognitive Domain*). New York. David McKay.

Ham, Sam. 1992. *Environmental Interpretation; A Practical Guide for People with Big Ideas and Small Budgets*. Golden, Colo.: North American Press.

Veverka, John A. 1994. *Interpretive Master Planning*. Helena, Mont.: Falcon Press Publishing.

CHAPTER 17 • # Disseminating Program Information

There's no need for a museum to reconfigure facts, techniques, or strategies whenever a new interpreter delivers a program. While each interpreter can and should use her individual talents and perspective, it is inefficient and counter-productive for a museum to constantly reinvent the wheel. An interpretive program is complete once all the information an interpreter needs to learn and deliver it has been compiled into an accessible and reusable format.

This chapter helps interpreters develop an institution-appropriate format for the written versions of each program. These program write-ups aid both current and future interpreters and establish an institutional history that can guide staff in the decades to come.

Each museum should develop its own format, but there are pieces of information that will be common to all program write-ups. Trainers should begin by asking trainees to recall their own experiences presenting new programs and discuss the kinds of information they found, or would have found, useful. Interpreters who are asked to consider their own needs are more likely to provide a comprehensive collection of information for others. Ask the group to make a list of the essential components of an effective write-up: "If you had to deliver a program one hour from now, what information would help you prepare effectively?"

Once the group's list has been recorded on a flip chart, compare it to Elements of Effective Program Write-Ups (overhead 17A) and discuss any elements not suggested by the group. Then review the Interpretive Program Write-Up Template (sample 17B), which provides one example of an effective program write-up. The organization of this template can be modified to meet the needs of the institution and its interpreters. To see other examples of program write-ups, go to www.visitordialogue.com.

Elements of Effective Program Write-Ups

Overhead 17A

➤ **Title** of the program

➤ Intended **length** and **format** of the program (e.g., 15-minute discovery cart demonstration; 30-minute exhibit tour)

➤ Target **audience**; who is the intended audience? (4th graders, seniors, general public, etc.)

➤ Recommended **location**(s) for the program (area where content will be connected to the collections)

➤ **Theme** and **messages** (big idea and supporting concepts)

➤ Bulleted program **objectives**; what do you want the visitor to learn, know, or do?

➤ List of **materials** and/or **props**; what materials will help to illustrate the messages?

➤ Program **set-up instructions**; how do you prepare for the program?

➤ Collection/list of **supporting resources** (articles, Web sites) for research questions

➤ Program **outline** (conversational script suggestions, transition ideas)

➤ Examples of conversational **introduction/closing**, if appropriate

➤ Clearly identified **tips/techniques for engaging visitors** (props, actions, questions)

➤ **Parting thoughts**; ideas that will keep visitors thinking about the theme after they leave

➤ **Frequently asked visitor questions**, with accurate responses

➤ **Others?**

Program Title:_____

Format: ____Structured ____Casual   **Target Audience:**_____

Description (tour, demo, drop-in)

Location: **Proposed Time(s):** _____

Theme:

Message 1:

Message 2:

Message 3:

Objectives:

Connection to mission/museum collection:

Program Preparation
Materials/Props:

Set-up Instructions: (attach set-up memo, if appropriate)

Program Delivery
Suggested key questions: (also specify use of prop or actions)

1.

2.

3.

4.

5.

(continues on next page)

Interpretive Program Write-up Template

Sample 17B

Sample conversational interactions with supporting info: (for casual interpretation)

<OR>

Program Outline: (for structured programs)
Introduction:

Body (addressing each message)

Conclusion:

Parting thoughts (ideas/take away items):

Program Support Information
Frequently asked questions/answers:

Reference list:

(Cite and attach copies of relevant articles, research materials.)

CHAPTER 18 • Interpretation Training Resources

This training manual aims to provide a comprehensive collection of resources and training tools to enable museums to create and deliver a customized training program. It should be considered a starting point, one that allows trainers to customize and adapt and thus meet the needs of the museum. Additional resources and networking with professional organizations can only improve the quality and effectiveness of the training program.

Listed here are books and articles that expand on the interpretation-related concepts found in this manual; organizations that may provide access to like-minded museums and professionals; and Web sites featuring educational and networking opportunities related to interpretation, visitor education, and informal learning. For updates to this list of resources, or to recommend a resource, please go to www.visitordialogue.com.

PUBLICATIONS

Baker, Ann C.; Jensen, Patricia J.; and Kolb, David A. 2002. *Conversational Learning: An Experiential Approach to Knowledge Creation*. Westport, Conn.: Quorum Books.

Barnett, Terry. 2003. *Interpreting Art: Reflecting, Wondering, and Responding*. New York: McGraw-Hill.

Beck, Larry, and Cable, Ted. 1998. *Interpretation for the 21st Century: Fifteen Guiding Principles for Interpreting Nature and Culture*. Champaign, Ill.: Sagamore Publishing.

Bloom, Benjamin S.; Mesia, Bertram B.; and Krathwohl, David R. 1964. *Taxonomy of Educational Objectives* (two vols: *The Affective Domain* and *The Cognitive Domain*). New York. David McKay.

Brochu, Lisa, and Merriman, Tim. 2002. *Personal Interpretation: Connecting Your Audiences to Heritage Resources*. Fort Collins, Colo.: InterpPress.

Bruner, Jerome. 1986. *Actual Minds, Possible Worlds*. Cambridge, Mass: Harvard University Press.

Bucy, David. 1998. *Planning for Success: Interpretive Planning Workshop Binder*, National Association of Interpretation Annual Meeting, Anchorage, Alaska.

Cable, T.; Knudson, D.; Udd, E.; and Stewart, D. 1987. "Attitude Changes as a Result of Exposure to Interpretive Messages." *Journal of Park Recreation Administration*. 5(1):47-60.

Clark, J. M., and Paivio, A. (1991). "Dual Coding Theory and Education." *Educational Psychology Review 3* (3), 149-170.

Csikszentmihalyi, M. (1990) *Flow: The Psychology of Optimal Experience*. New York: Harper and Row.

Dahlen, D.; Larsen, D.; Weber, S.; and Fudge, R. 1996. "The Process of Interpretation: Fulfilling the Mission through Interpretive Competencies." *1996 Interpretive Sourcebook: Proceedings of the National Interpreters Workshop*: 106-108.

Dale, Edgar. 1969. *Audio-Visual Methods in Teaching*. (3d ed.) Austin, Tex.: Holt, Rinehaert, Winston.

Dewey, John. 1938. *Experience and Education*. New York: Collier Books.

Diamond, Judy. 1999. *Practical Evaluation Guide: Tools for Museums and Other Informal Educational Settings*. Walnut Creek, Calif.: AltaMira Press.

Dierking, Lynn D.; Luke, Jessica J.; Foat, Kathryn A.; and Adelman, Leslie. 2001. "The Family and Free-Choice Learning." *Museum News*. November/December.

Falk, John H., and Dierking, Lynn. 1992. *The Museum Experience*. Washington, D.C.: Whalesback Books.

———. 2000. *Learning from Museums: Visitor Experiences and the Making of Meaning*. Walnut Creek, Calif.: AltaMira Press.

———. 2002. *Lessons Without Limit: How Free-Choice Learning Is Transforming Education*. Walnut Creek, Calif.: AltaMira Press.

The Docent Handbook. 2001. Indianapolis: National Docent Symposium Council and Design Printing Company.

Gardner, Howard. 1991. *The Unschooled Mind: How Children Think and How Schools Should Teach*. New York: Basic Books.

Gartenhaus, Alan. 1991. *Minds in Motion: Using Museums to Expand Creative Thinking*. San Francisco: Caddo Gap Press

———. 2001. *Questioning Art: An Inquiry Approach to Teaching Art Appreciation*. Virgina Beach: The Donning Company Publishers.

Grinder, Alison, and McCoy, E. Sue. 1985. *The Good Guide*. Tucson, Ariz.: Ironwood Publishing.

Ham, Sam. 1992. *Environmental Interpretation*. Golden, Colo.: North American Press.

Hein, George. 1991. "The Museum and the Needs of People." Proceedings of the International Committee of Museum Educators Conference. Posted to Association of Science and Technology Centers' Web site: ww.astc.org

———. 1995. "The Constructivist Museum." *Journal of Education in Museums*. 16:21-23.

———. 1998. *Learning in the Museum*. New York: Routledge.

——— and Alexander, Mary. 1998. *Museums: Places of Learning*. Washington, D.C.: American Association of Museums.

Honig, Maryke. 2000. *Making Your Garden Come Alive; Environmental Interpretation in Botanical Gardens*. Cape Town, South Africa: CTP Press.

Hooper-Greenhill, Eileen, ed. 1999. *The Educational Role of the Museum*. New York: · Routledge.

Knudson, D.; Cable, T.; and Beck, L. 1995. *Interpretation of Cultural and Natural Resources*. State College, Pa.: Venture Publishing, Inc.

Larsen, David L., ed. 2003. *Meaningful Interpretation: How to Connect Hearts and Minds to Places, Objects, and Other Resources*. Fort Washington, Pa.: Eastern National.

Leinhardt, Gaea; Crowley, Kevin; and Knutson, Karen, eds. 2002. *Learning Conversations in Museums*. Mahwah, N.J.: Lawrence Earlbaum Associates, Inc., Publishers.

Levy, Barbara Abramoff; Lloyd, Sandra McKenzie; and Schreiber, Susan Porter. 2001. *Great Tours! Thematic Tours and Guide Training for Historic Sites*. Walnut Creek, Calif.: AltaMira Press.

Lewis, William J. 1980. *Interpreting for Park Visitors*. Philadelphia: Eastern Acorn Press.

————. 1994. *Reaching for Excellence: The Process of Interpretive Critiquing* (video). Stonington, Conn.: Interpretation Publication and Resource Center.

Loomis, R. 1996. "How Do We Know What the Visitor Knows? Learning from Interpretation." *Journal of Interpretation Research*. 1(1): 39-45.

Machalis, G., and Field, D., eds. 1992. *On Interpretation*. Corvallis: Oregon State University Press.

Marino, Margie, and Koke, Judy. 2003. "Face to Face: Examining Educational Staff's Impact on Visitors." *ASTC Dimensions* (Association of Science and Technology Centers). January/February.

Maslow, A. 1954. *Motivation and Personality*. New York: Harper and Row Publishers, Inc.

McLean, Kathleen. 1996. *Planning for People in Museum Exhibits*. Washington, D.C.: Association of Science and Technology Centers.

Mills, Enos. 1920. *Adventures of a Nature Guide and Essays on Interpretation*. Friendship, Wis.: New Past Press.

Moll, L. C., ed. 1990. *Vygotsky and Education*. Cambridge, Mass.: Cambridge University Press.

Paris, Scott G., ed. 2002. *Perspectives on Object-Based Learning in Museums*. Mahwah, N.J.: Lawrence Earlbaum Associates, Inc., Publishers.

Parfitt, Phil. 1997. *Organizational Development of the Education Department— Conversation*. Unpublished Education Plan for the Peggy Notebaert Nature Museum of the Chicago Academy of Sciences.

Parsons, Chris. 1996. "Starting an Interpreter Evaluation Program." *Legacy Magazine,* March/April.

Perry, Deborah, and Morrissey, Kristine. 2002. Designing for Conversation pre-conference workshop and materials, American Association of Museums, Dallas.

Piaget, Jean. 1964. "Development and Learning." *Journal of Research in Science Teaching,* 3: 176-186. New York: Wiley and Sons.

Pine, B. Joseph, and Gilmore, James H. 1999. *The Experience Economy*. Boston: Harvard Business School Press.

Pitman, Bonnie, ed. 1999. *Presence of Mind: Museums and the Spirit of Learning*. Washington, D.C.: American Association of Museums.

Regnier, Kathleen; Gross, Michael; and Zimmerman, Ron. 1994. *The Interpreter's Guidebook*. Madison, Wis.: UW-SP Foundation Press, Inc.

Roberts, Lisa. 1997. *From Knowledge to Narrative: Education and the Changing Museum*. Washington, D.C.: Smithsonian Institution Press.

Russell, Bob. 1999. "Experienced-based Learning Theories." *The Informal Learning Review*, 35 March/April: 1-4.

Sachetello-Sawyer, Bonnie, et al. 2002. *Adult Museums Programs; Designing Meaningful Experiences*. Walnut Creek, Calif.: AltaMira Press.

Screven, C. G. 1999. *Visitor Studies Bibliography and Abstracts*. (4th ed.) Chicago: Screven and Associates. (Order via e-mail at screv@att.net or by calling 773-752-5615.)

Serrell, Beverly. 1996. *Exhibit Labels; An Interpretive Approach*. Walnut Creek, Calif.: AltaMira Press.

Sharpe, Grant W., ed. 1982. *Interpreting the Environment*. (2d ed.) New York: Macmillan.

Singer, Elayna. 2000. "Planning Success." *Public Garden*. July/August/September: 16-19.

Tilden, Freeman. 1957. *Interpreting Our Heritage*. Chapel Hill: University of North Carolina Press.

Veverka, John A. 1994. *Interpretive Master Planning*. Helena, Mont.: Falcon Press Publishing.

Vygotsky, L. S. 1962. *Thought and Language*. Cambridge, Mass.: MIT Press.

Weil, Stephen E. 2002. *Making Museums Matter*. Washington, D.C.: Smithsonian Institution Press.

ORGANIZATIONS

American Association of Botanical Gardens and Arboreta (AABGA)
351 Longwood Rd.
Kennett Square, PA 19348
610-925-2500, 610-925-2700 fax
www.aabga.org

American Association of Museums (AAM)
1575 Eye St. N.W., Suite 400
Washington, DC 20005
202-289-1818, 202-289-6578 fax
www.aam-us.org
National Interpretation Project: www.aam-us.org/NIPoverview.htm

American Association of State and Local History (AASLH)
1717 Church St.
Nashville, TN 37203
615-320-3203, 615-327-9013 fax
www.aaslh.org

American Zoo and Aquarium Association (AZA)
8403 Colesville Rd., Suite 710
Silver Spring, MD 20910-3314
301-562-0777, 301-562-0888 fax
www.aza.org

Association for Living Historical Farms & Agricultural Museums (ALHFAM)
8774 Rte. 45 N.W.
North Bloomfield, Ohio 44450
216-685-4410
www.alhfam.org

Association of Children's Museums (ACM)
1300 L St. N.W., Suite 975
Washington, DC 20005
202-898-1080, 202-898-1086 fax
www.childrensmuseums.org

Association of Science-Technology Centers (ASTC)
1025 Vermont Ave. N.W., Suite 500
Washington, DC 20005-3516
202-783-7200, 202-783-7207 fax
www.astc.org

Association for Volunteer Administration (AVA)
P.O. Box 32092
Richmond, VA 23294
804-346-2266, 804-346-3318 fax
www.avaintl.org

Group for Education in Museums (GEM)
www.gem.org.uk
The Group for Education in Museum promotes the importance of learning through museums and galleries. It is based in the United Kingdom but has members around the world.

Interpretation Canada
c/o Kerry Woods Nature Center
6300 45th Ave.
Red Deer, Alberta, Canada, T4N 3M4
604 648-8757 fax
E-mail: membership@interpcan.ca
www.interpcan.ca
Offers regular enrichment training and conferences/networking opportunities for interpreters.

Museum Education Roundtable (MER)
www.mer-online.org
Museum Education Roundtable is an active network encouraging leadership, development, scholarship, and personal development among educators and museum professionals.

National Association for Interpretation (NAI)
P.O. Box 2246
Fort Collins, CO 80522
888-900-8283, 970-484-8179 fax
www.interpnet.org
NAI is dedicated to the advancement of the interpretation profession. Annual conferences and ongoing certification training programs are available for professional development.

National Park Service (NPS)
Stephen T. Mather Employee Development Center
Interpretive Development Program
P.O. Box 77
Harpers Ferry, WV 25425-0077
www.nps.gov/idp/interp/index.htm
www.nps.org
The National Park Service has extensive interpretive training opportunities for government employees.

National Storytelling Network
101 Courthouse Square
Jonesborough, TN 37659
800-525-4514, 423-753-9331 fax
www.storynet.org
Serves as resource to individuals and organizations that use the power of storytelling in all its forms.

Visitor Studies Association (VSA)
P.O. Box 470845
Aurora, CO 80047-0845
303-337-4301, 303-753-3247 fax
www.visitorstudies.org
The Visitor Studies Association (VSA) is a nonprofit professional organization dedicated to the proposition that museums, in addition to meeting their own organizational objectives, should be effective meeting the expectations, needs, and interests of visitors.

ADDITIONAL RESOURCES

Active Learning Site
www.active-learning-site.com
This site provides research-based resources designed to help educators implement active learning in their classrooms.

Acorn Naturalists
17821 E. 17th St., #103
P.O. Box 2423
Tustin, CA 92781-2423
800-422-8886, 800-452-2802 fax
www.acornnaturalists.com
Excellent resource for acquiring nature-related props and books to complement training and programs.

The Docent Educator
P.O. Box 2080
Kamuela, HI 96743-2080
808-885-7728, 808-885-8315 fax
This is a subscription-based publication written by volunteers and the staff who work with them.

National Docent Symposium Council
Mail Boxes Etc., Box 412
2342 Shattuck Ave.
Berkley, CA 94704
www.docents.net
This is a volunteer organization dedicated to providing docent education and the exchange of ideas through a National Docent Symposium, held every two years at host institutions in the United States and Canada.

The Informal Learning Review (publication of Informal Learning Experiences, Inc.)
P.O. Box 42328
Washington, DC 20015
202-362-5823, 202-362-3596 fax
www.informallearning.com
Valuable resource for current trends in informal learning techniques and research.

Informal Science

www.informalscience.org

Informal Science promotes and advances the field of informal learning in science and other domains. This site allows interactive searches of references of research literature on informal learning in museums, on the Web, and beyond.

Institute for Inquiry (housed at the Exploratorium in San Francisco)

www.exploratorium.edu/IFI/resources/index.html

Resources focused on inquiry-based learning.

Museum Learning Collaborative

www.museumlearning.org

An online resource established to further theoretically driven research on learning in museums.

Museum Studies Reference Library of the Smithsonian Institution Library

www.sil.si.edu/libraries/mrc-hp.htm

Includes materials that are difficult to find or not indexed, including *Journal of Museum Education*, American Law Institute-American Bar Association annual seminar proceedings, AAM annual meeting tapes, and museum-related theses and dissertations.

Visual Understanding in Education (VUE)

Visual Thinking Strategies (VTS)

www.vue.org

Source of supplemental research and published curriculum for teaching elementary school students about art.

CHAPTER 19 • **Glossary**

Behavioral Objective: "What do I want visitors to do?" If we can inspire a visitor to take action, we have truly succeeded. When we encourage visitors to interact with the collections or become involved in the mission, we are making personal connections. Public involvement translates into long-term success.

Captive Audience: Audiences who are required to or feel they must pay attention to a program, regardless of whether they are engaged.

Collection/Event Context: "What is the larger setting for the program? What is the collection or event about?" The context typically is determined before the interpretive programs are developed and is usually evident from the program's title (e.g., "Modern Art: 1950 to the Present," "Fall Harvest Festival," "Africa Explored: A Quest to Uncover History"). The context establishes priorities and parameters that reinforce the goals of the site or event. It refers to the expectations created for visitors through text and/or tone of the title and promotional materials.

Conclusion: The program conclusion should summarize your messages and refer back to the theme. This may be an opportunity to have visitors share what they learned to reinforce the messages.

Conversation: An informal exchange of ideas, facts, values, opinions, feelings, etc. This can refer to an internal exchange or one between two or more people.

Conversational Script: An example of how questions, actions, or props might be used to engage visitors in message-based conversations. Because conversations can never truly be scripted, these serve only as suggestions of ways interpreters can initiate an interaction and should provide supplemental information to support a dialogue on the given message.

Emotional Objective: "What do I want visitors to feel?" Accounting for emotions is an important part of the decision-making process. If we want to influence attitudes or behavior, we must strive to reach visitors emotionally. By considering how we want visitors to feel, we are more likely to create experiences that will influence their actions and the knowledge they gain.

Intangible Concepts: How does something make an individual feel? What emotions or experiences does it relate to? Are there experiences someone might associate with the concept/object that could be included in the program? These abstract concepts are important for making emotional connections.

Interactive/Illustrative Tools: These tools should be tangible opportunities (props) that invite visitors to use their senses to experience the message. Using props provides a focal point that the visitor can associate with the message, and thus increases the potential for a meaningful and relevant experience.

Interpreter: any individual who serves in a front-line role and facilitates positive and educational visitor experiences.

Interpretation: Interpretation is conversation, guided interaction, or any communication that enriches the visitor experience by making meaningful connections between the messages and collections of our institution and the intellectual and emotional world of the visitor.

Interpretive Program Worksheet: A tool that helps interpreters brainstorm content and delivery strategies for increasing opportunities for conversation and connections with visitors.

Introduction: The beginning of a program must hook the audience into participating and communicate the theme. Interpreters can build expectations by referring to the messages here, but the full description of the message should unfold as a part of a compelling program.

Key Questions: Questions used throughout the program to engage visitors by asking them to process, compare, or internalize information. Not all of the questions need to be answered!

Learning Location: "Where will this program be experienced?" Identifying where the program will take place can increase effectiveness by allowing interpreters to capitalize on the area's strengths and avoid its pitfalls (e.g., overcrowding, noise).

Learning Objective: "What do I want visitors to *know*?"
This objective is focused on having visitors be able to recall, list, or describe facts or items after a program is completed. Determining which facts you want visitors to retain is valuable, but we are more likely to be make connections if we also identify how we want the visitor to feel and act after the program. (Veverka, 1994)

Messages:

Messages offer supporting "evidence"—stories, experiences, concepts—that help to illustrate the theme. Limiting the number of messages to three increases the impact and retention of more specific ideas and helps avoid confusion. The desired facts, emotions, or behaviors determined in the objectives above should be integrated into the messages. Specifically: "If I want visitors to understand the theme, it is important for them to *know/feel/do. . . .* "

Parting Thoughts: This aspect of the program reinforces the "take-away" element of all programs. It can be simple statements, questions, or hand-outs (sheets, stickers, rewards) that encourage visitors to continue thinking about the message after they leave the museum.

Program Theme: The theme is the "big idea" or overriding concept you want visitors to take away with them; it is a general statement that encompasses all the elements of the program. You can formulate the theme by completing this sentence: "If there is one thing I want the visitor to remember about this site/topic, it is that. . . . "

Program Title: The title for the program should be considered only after previous exercises have been completed. It should capture the program's uniqueness and excitement, build visitor expectations, and suggest the reward of attending.

Program Topics: "What is this program about?"
Program topics are the subject matter that shapes the theme. Topics (e.g.; Oregon history, basket weaving, forensic science, pollination) answer the question, "What information should be conveyed to visitors?" Topics are fragments, not complete thoughts or sentences. (Ham, 1992)

Program Write-up: A comprehensive, yet accessible format for delivering written directions and background information to support the successful delivery of an interpretive program; similar to a lesson plan for educational program in an informal learning setting.

Proposed Time(s): "When will the program occur?"
The time of the program can influence its content and nature. The ideal time for a program is based on the visitation patterns of the target audience. For example, if the desired audience is school groups, the program should be offered between 10 a.m. and 2 p.m. The proposed time(s) can specify start times for a structured tour, such as 3 p.m., or indicate a range of time when casual interpretation might occur, such as "between 1 and 3 p.m."

Public Perception Considerations: Be aware of what the public may be thinking; everyone brings emotional baggage. Read the papers and understand current events that may influence visitor opinions, fears, and feelings.

Tangible Concepts: How does something look, smell, feel (texture), etc.? What is (or can be) known by everyone about the concept/object through observation? These concepts help visitors make intellectual connections.

Target Audience: "Whom is this program for?" The target audience is either the people who are already coming to your museum (e.g., families, school groups) or the people you would like to attract through a special program (e.g., Girl Scouts, senior tour groups).

Theme: See program theme.

Universal Meanings: Concepts or ideas connected to the interpretive program that relate to everyday life and often reference family, change, history, work, reward, money, etc. Referring to these meanings in your dialogue can help make program content relevant to everyone in the audience.

REFERENCES

Ham, Sam. 1992. *Environmental Interpretation*. Golden, Colo.: North American Press.

Veverka, John A. 1994. *Interpretive Master Planning*. Helena, Mont.: Falcon Press Publishing.

CHAPTER 20 • Training Tools

TRAINING TOOLS AS HANDOUTS

In addition to serving as teaching tools for the trainer, the following forms can be photocopied and distributed to trainees to supplement training.

Module 1

Module 2

Module 3

FINDING A TRAINING TOOL

The lists that follow are intended to help readers differentiate among the types of training tools discussed in this book. Thus, if you cannot find the document you need in one category, you can easily search through another.

Exercises

Overheads

The Author

Mary Kay Cunningham is an interpretive specialist with more than 10 years of experience working with museums and other educational sites to improve the visitor learning experience. Her company, Dialogue, works to facilitate meaningful connections between institutions and their visitors through interpretive training, programming, and institutional planning. In addition to serving as a guest lecturer at the University of Oregon and regularly presenting at professional conferences, she has published numerous pieces on interpretation in *Public Garden*, the journal of the American Association of Botanical Gardens and Arboreta; *Legacy*, the magazine of the National Association of Interpretation; and *ASTC Dimensions*, the journal of the Association of Science and Technology Centers. She earned a graduate degree in environmental interpretation at Northeastern Illinois University and an undergraduate degree in communications and environmental studies at Marquette University. She lives in Portland, Oreg.

Index

Page numbers in italics indicate exercises, overheads, worksheets, etc.

P

Q

R

S

T